How Libraries AND Librarians Help

A Guide to Identifying User-Centered Outcomes

Joan C. Durrance and **Karen E. Fisher**

with Marian Bouch Hinton

American Library Association

Chicago   2005

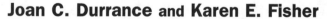

Design and composition by ALA Editions in Electra and Franklin Gothic using QuarkXPress 5.0 on a PC platform

Printed on 50-pound white offset, a pH-neutral stock, and bound in 10-point cover stock by McNaughton & Gunn

The paper used in this publication meets the minimum requirements of American National Standard for Information Sciences—Permanence of Paper for Printed Library Materials, ANSI Z39.48-1992. ∞

Library of Congress Cataloging-in-Publication Data
Durrance, Joan C.
    How libraries and librarians help : assessing outcomes in your library / Joan C. Durrance, Karen E. Fisher ; with Marian Bouch Hinton.
        p.   cm.
    Includes bibliographical references and index.
    ISBN 0-8389-0892-6 (alk. paper)
    1. Libraries—Evaluation. 2. Libraries—United States—Evaluation. 3. Public services (Libraries)—Evaluation. 4. Public services (Libraries)—United States—Evaluation. 5. Public libraries—United States—Evaluation—Case studies. 6. Libraries and community—United States. I. Fisher, Karen E., 1966– II. Hinton, Marian Bouch. III. Title.
    Z685.85D87 2005
    027—dc22   2004022581

Printed in the United States of America

09   08   07   06   05   5   4   3   2   1

CONTENTS

FIGURES   *v*

PREFACE   *vii*

ACKNOWLEDGMENTS   *ix*

Part I

Outcomes: A New Way to Show
How Libraries and Librarians Help

1   The Urgent Need to Tell the Library Story More Effectively   *3*

2   Outcomes: An Approach That Shows the Value of Libraries   *12*

3   The "How Libraries and Librarians Help" Outcome Model:
Applying Contextual Approaches to Outcome Evaluation   *24*

Part II

How to Measure and Predict the Outcomes
of Your Own Library Programs and Services

4   Step One
Getting Started: Preparing to Conduct an Outcomes Study   *33*

5   Step Two
Collecting Data for Outcomes: Approaches and Tools   *36*

6   Step Three
Analyzing Outcomes Data   *64*

7   Step Four
        Maximizing the Results of Your Outcomes Study   *71*

8   Predicting Outcomes: Outcome Measures as a Planning Tool   *84*
            RHEA JOYCE RUBIN

Part III

Putting Outcomes to Use: How Libraries
Contribute to Individuals and the Community

9   Ripples of Impact: Washtenaw Literacy Program Outcomes   *93*
            MARIA SOUDEN AND SARAH WOODEN

10 Empowering Youth: Outcomes of Public Libraries'
        Youth Technology Programs   *114*

11 Strengthening Community: Outcomes of Community
        Information Services   *136*

12 Putting the Pieces Together: An Outcome Study of the Ypsilanti
        District Library's Senior Deposit Collection Program   *150*
            DANA WALKER AND JEANIE FISHER

INDEX   *179*

FIGURES

1-1   Showing How Reading Makes a Difference   *9*

2-1   Categories of Outcomes Compiled
      by the Annie E. Casey Foundation   *14*

2-2   Selected List of Candidate Public Library Outcomes Identified by "How
      Libraries and Librarians Help"   *16*

3-1   The United Way Outcome Model   *24*

3-2   The "How Libraries and Librarians Help" Outcome Model   *25*

3-3   Ripples of Impact of a Basic Literacy Program   *29*

4-1   Potential Program Impacts of the Queens Borough Public Library's
      New Americans and Adult Learner Programs   *35*

5-1   Community Network User Survey   *51*

5-2   Data Collection Plan for the Queens Borough Public Library's
      New Americans and Adult Learner Programs   *61*

6-1   Sample Outcomes Table for the Peninsula Library System's
      Community Information Program   *68*

7-1   Matching Internal Audiences and Outcomes   *76*

7-2   Matching External Audiences and Outcomes   *76*

7-3   Determining Dissemination Strategies   *77*

7-4   Outcomes Graphic for the Queens Borough Public Library's
      New Americans and Adult Learner Programs   *79*

7-5   Outcomes Graphic for the Peninsula Library System's Community
      Information Program   *80*

7-6   Matching Outcomes against Goals   *81*
7-7   Resource (Re)allocation Plan for the Queens Borough Public Library's
          New Americans and Adult Learner Programs   *82*

9-1   Sample Learner Interview Questions   *97*
9-2   Sample Tutor Interview Questions   *98*
9-3   Sample Staff Focus Group Questions   *98*
9-4   Ripples of Impact: Successive Outcome Levels   *100*
9-5   Basic Washtenaw Literacy Program Outcomes   *100*

10-1 Outcomes of the "Wired for Youth" Community
          Technology Program   *120*
10-2 Candidate Outcomes of the Austin Public Library's
          "Wired for Youth" Program   *121*
10-3 Outcomes of the CIAO Program   *125*
10-4 Candidate Outcomes of the Flint Public Library's CIAO Program   *127*
10-5 Evaluation Outcomes for the Haines Dragonfly Project   *132*

11-1 Community Information Program Outcomes for Human Service
          Organizations   *141*
11-2 Service Activities and Candidate Outcomes of the Peninsula Library
          System's Community Information Program   *147*

12-1 The Outcomes Puzzle   *161*
12-2 Outcomes of the Ypsilanti District Library's Senior Deposit Collection
          Program   *167*

PREFACE

This book provides information professionals with a user-centered, how-to-do-it guide to identifying, assessing, and communicating the manifold and rich outcomes of library services. In addition, it makes two unique contributions to the literature of outcome assessment by

1. addressing the urgent need to more effectively tell the "library story" by framing outcomes within their holistic contexts; and
2. bringing outcomes to life by sharing the experiences of librarians who learned how they help people in their communities—often in ways they did not expect.

This book is divided into three parts.

Part 1, "Outcomes: A New Way to Show How Libraries and Librarians Help," focuses on the decades-old problem faced by librarians: their inability to inform people of the contributions that libraries and librarians make in the community. The ability to effectively assess and communicate outcomes is an important addition to the toolkit of librarians. In part 1 we explain the importance of outcomes and introduce the How Libraries and Librarians Help (HLLH) outcome model that we developed as part of our Institute of Museum and Library Services-supported National Leadership Grant.

Part 2, "How to Measure and Predict the Outcomes of Your Own Library Programs and Services," shows how effective outcome evaluation can be conducted in four steps. Throughout part 2, we illustrate each step with examples from the experience of libraries we have worked with, such as the Queens Borough (N.Y.) Public Library. The four steps, each of which constitutes a chapter in part 2, are briefly described as follows.

"Step One: Getting Started: Preparing to Conduct an Outcomes Study" asks librarians to identify the specific services that they wish to evaluate and those services' varied stakeholders, as well as to brainstorm about possible outcomes while gaining an understanding of the context of the service and evaluation process.

"Step Two: Collecting Data for Outcomes: Approaches and Tools" focuses on approaches for collecting data from the users themselves—in their own words whenever possible—because data collected in this way provide the richness needed to tell the library story from the user's perspective.

"Step Three: Analyzing Outcomes Data" provides approaches for organizing and making sense of the valuable user-focused responses gathered in step 2. These approaches are key to identifying a set of user-focused outcomes.

"Step Four: Maximizing the Results of Your Outcomes Study" identifies a variety of ways to use and present data on outcomes both internally and in the community.

Rhea Rubin, a well-known consultant and presenter on a variety of evaluation and library development topics, contributes a strong fifth chapter to part 2 about ways to predict outcomes and to use outcome measurement as a planning tool.

Part 3, "Putting Outcomes to Use," shows what can be learned from using this holistic and contextual approach to outcome assessment. In this part we document how library programs actually contribute to individuals and communities through the experience of four different kinds of user-focused programs. Part 3 begins with "Ripples of Impact," the story of the Washtenaw Literacy program, whose participants not only made clear learning gains but also felt better about themselves, became stronger contributors to their families and workplaces, and made contributions to their communities as a result of their participation in the program. "Empowering Youth" is a powerful chapter on outcomes that accrued to youths who attended after-school technology programs in three communities— Flint (Mich.), Austin (Tex.), and Haines (Alaska)—starting, of course, with technology skill gains, but extending to social skills, a new excitement for learning, and in some youths, new civic engagement skills. "Strengthening Community" shows how the outcomes of a 25-year-old community information program accrued to both the clients of social service agencies and to the community. "Putting the Pieces Together" uses the words of frail elderly persons in residential facilities who were recipients of senior deposit collections to present the outcomes of this service, which included providing mental sustenance and sustaining a sense of identity.

The chapters in part 3 thus bring to life the process presented in part 2. These chapters show that outcome assessment can, as suggested in part 1, give librarians the tools they need to communicate how libraries and librarians help—how they make strong contributions to the lives of children and adults, to community organizations, and to the fabric of the community.

ACKNOWLEDGMENTS

This book has been several years in the making. It would not have been possible without the Institute of Museum and Library Services (IMLS), which generously supported "How Libraries and Librarians Help" with a National Leadership Grant in 2000.

The rich examples that we relied upon to develop our framework were drawn from excellent libraries that generously opened their doors to us. We wish to thank the staff of the Flint Public Library and the Austin Public Library, where we examined youth-focused community technology programs; the King County Library System, which let us evaluate its "Voices around the Rim" public programming; the Peninsula Library System, which helped us examine its Community Information Program; and the Queens Borough Public Library, which helped us understand its numerous programs designed to serve immigrants—in particular the New Americans Program and the Adult Learner Program. At all of these sites we learned from the users of these services that the library helps them in ways that even devoted staff members didn't fully understand.

A dedicated group of graduate-student research assistants at the University of Michigan and the University of Washington made strong contributions to collecting and analyzing the data, writing up the results, contributing to the project website, and helping us create the web-based Outcomes Toolkit. These research assistants include Bryn Martin Cope, Peter Emonds-Banfield, Chris Hamilton, Marian Bouch Hinton, Michael Jourdan, Eunice Kua, Chic Naumer, Erica Olsen, Mike Pruzan, Karen Scheuerer, Maria Souden, Vishant Shaw, Nicolette Sosulski, Anne Turner, Tammara Turner, Kent Unruh, Dana Walker, and Kate Zoellner.

In order to test our HLLH outcome evaluation approach, we held a workshop at the Information School of the University of Washington in Seattle in October 2001, which was supported by IMLS with additional funding from the Alliance for Community Technology. Fourteen participants, representing libraries in ten states, were selected through a competitive process. They came from a variety of communities looking for approaches for determining the outcomes of economic development and job information programs, an immigrant service, after-school technology programs for teens, literacy services, a consumer health service, services targeted for Native Americans (carried out by the Pacific Northwest division of the National Library of Medicine), a distributed community network, and two state agencies. The workshop and the resulting interactions with participants prodded us to tweak the HLLH approach. We appreciate the participants' contributions; the "Empowering Youth" chapter in part 3 incorporates an outcome study done by Ann Myren, one of the participants in the workshop, and her colleagues at the Haines Borough Public Library in Haines, Alaska.

The graduate courses that we designed and taught on outcome assessment at the University of Michigan and the University of Washington resulted in several additional studies based on our HLLH approach (and thus further testing of the model). Two of the studies, "Ripples of Impact" and "Putting the Pieces Together," are included in this book, and we appreciate the contributions of all students in these classes.

Marian Bouch Hinton deserves special mention in this preface. Over many months she made major writing and editing contributions to the development of this book and cheerfully kept the coauthors on target.

Finally, a web tool of our HLLH approach known as the Outcomes Toolkit contains further overviews and sample data-collection instruments, which were also tested in real-world settings and can be used as models on which to base further contextual outcome studies. Our only caveat is that you should remember that no two services are alike and that all instruments should reflect your own situation. The Outcomes Toolkit is available at our IBEC (Information Behavior in Everyday Contexts) website at http://ibec.ischool.washington.edu/, which we hope you will visit and use to keep in touch. We want to hear from you.

JOAN C. DURRANCE
KAREN E. FISHER

Outcomes

*A New Way to Show How
Libraries and Librarians Help*

The Urgent Need to Tell
the Library Story More Effectively

Libraries: Integral and Ignored

By and large, experts and decision makers have failed to recognize the contributions that libraries and librarians make to society. Libraries have been overlooked in landmark studies of societal institutions, ignored in major government reports, omitted from important legislation, and not included in foundation priorities.[1] This problem goes back at least to the early decades of the twentieth century. Commenting on the absence of libraries in a major study of American life in 1932, the president of the American Library Association (ALA) at the time was quoted as saying, "What have we done or not done that this can be so? . . . Why is it that we have not impressed ourselves, as an important and essential institution, upon the governing body or upon intelligent authors and scholars? Is it in the very nature of our work that it should be so, or is it in ourselves?"[2]

More recently, Robert Putnam of *Bowling Alone* fame spoke at the Annual Conference of the ALA. Putnam, who had analyzed scores of factors and institutions that contribute to or limit social capital, failed to even mention libraries either in his book or in his address to librarians.[3] Some in the audience, as could be expected, were stunned. One educator, Jean Preer, argued (in an article addressed to librarians) that libraries contribute to most of the conditions that Putnam predicts will create a "more engaged civic and community life," including stimulating the civic engagement of young people, fostering tolerance, arts and cultural activities, and activities that inform citizens.[4] Preer asserts that for more than a century, public libraries have worked to create an informed citizenry and to build community—only to be ignored.

The response to being ignored or overlooked has often been hand-wringing and self-reproaches among librarians, as well as faulting of the experts, the legislators, or the foundations for their ignorance. And there is still much discussion of these issues within the fold. The truth is that librarians have failed to explain to those outside the field what contributions they and their institutions actually make to society at large. Indeed, until now librarians have lacked both approaches and appropriate tools, and, perhaps, the culture, to show the contributions that librarians make every day in their communities. Peggy Rudd, director of the Texas State Library and Archives Commission, has commented:

> Those of us who have committed our life's work to the improvement of libraries are continually frustrated with our lack of ability to effectively "tell the library story." While it would be more convenient if the worth of libraries was simply accepted on faith by university presidents, county commissioners, city managers, and school boards, that is frequently not the case.[5]

Increasing Demands for Accountability

Several converging factors—including pressure (and encouragement) from the federal government, increasingly user-focused mission statements and reporting mechanisms, and funded research such as that which served as the basis for this book—have helped move the field toward an ability to articulate library impact. These factors mean that librarians can use the approaches we have devised to identify and articulate the contributions of their own libraries to society.

Pressure from the federal government on all agencies to assure accountability has resulted in considerable activity, first at the federal level, and, more recently, at the state and local levels of government. Governments no longer trust agencies to "do the right thing." They now demand proof of accountability of all agencies.[6] These demands have helped to focus attention in the library field (and other fields as well) on developing tools and approaches that can show worth.

The Institute of Museum and Library Services (IMLS) has charged librarians to show how libraries and librarians help society by reporting concrete "benefits to people: specifically, achievements or changes in skill, knowledge, attitude, behavior, condition, or life status" that come as a result of library services.[7] Furthermore, IMLS has warned that "if museums and libraries do not take the responsibility for developing their own set of credible indicators, they risk having someone else do it for them."[8] Lastly, IMLS has both funded research aimed at helping to solve the problem and has developed a variety of approaches that foster the use of outcomes in evaluation.[9]

This book builds on research funded by IMLS. It builds, as well, on the work that has been done over the decades by researchers who have focused on information behavior—how people need, seek, and use information, and the barriers that stand in their way—and on the work of those who have provided librarians with a variety of planning and management tools, most notably, output measures. For years, librarians have calculated output measures as numerical depictions of institutional productivity. But output measures alone cannot capture the range of "benefits to people" that could, in aggregate, substantiate a library's impact on its community. In the hands of librarians willing to complement outputs with outcomes in evaluating services, this book will serve as a tool to educate members of the public, decision makers, and thought leaders. It will also be a vehicle for developing more effective user-focused services.

Mission Statements: Libraries' Promises to, and for, the Community

Public library mission statements reflect the desire of library planners for their libraries to serve a vital role in their community. These statements are increasingly framed with a focus on the library's contributions to community life and to the life of each person who lives there.

The mission statement of the Providence (R.I.) Public Library, winner of a national award for library service, is framed with the community as its center:

> Operating from a reputation for excellence and a history of community investment, the Providence Public Library, a national leader, assures that everyone— every child and adult, every citizen and newcomer, every individual and group, regardless of economic position, neighborhood or native language—will have an opportunity to grow intellectually, to nurture creativity and to achieve their potential. The Library will offer informational and educational services and recreation in both traditional and innovative ways that anticipate the needs of its growing and diverse populations.[10]

Increasingly, mission statements show that public libraries seek to

> "promote the development of independent, self-confident, and literate citizens"[11]

> "enhance the personal development" of citizens "by seeking to meet their informational needs, recognizing the benefits to the community of a well-informed citizenry, the individual's capacity for self-improvement, the worth of each person and the need for human dignity"[12]

Many public library annual reports open with mission statements such as these, which can lay the groundwork for more effective indicators of the impact that public libraries make in their communities. As Nelson notes, the purpose of the mission statement is "to inform the community about the library's priorities in clear and easily understood terms."[13] According to Wallace, "a good mission statement should make us feel our corner of the world is a better place because of the library. And it should make everyone connected with it feel proud."[14]

Library planners have a vision of meeting community needs, and they articulate this vision in the library's mission statement. A library's service model grows from the library's vision of its role and the articulation of this vision in the mission statement. The Public Library Association (PLA) has developed a set of tools aimed at helping librarians move from a vision to a service model with its goals, objectives, and activities.[15] Until now, public libraries have lacked the ability to show how—from the perspective of the community—library services effectively carry out their missions. The primary evaluation tool at a librarian's disposal, up until now, has been *Output Measures for Public Libraries*.[16] PLA leaders, recognizing the need to build upon output measures for outcome evaluation, are now recommending looking outside the field for assistance.[17]

Building on Output Measures

Librarians have since the 1980s relied on "outputs" as indicators of libraries' contributions to their communities. These measures were developed in response to the need to move public libraries beyond a focus on inputs and a time-honored, but limiting, focus on circulation. The output measures currently being used by most public librarians were identified by a group of librarians and researchers in the early 1980s (one of the authors of this book served on the ALA committee that originally identified and defined these measures). These measures were quickly adopted as those that reflected progressive library services, and became the output measures "canon." Developers added, to circulation counts, several library use and materials use measures, programming measures, materials access measures, and basic reference measures.[18]

Public libraries, state agencies, and the federal government have come to rely on *Output Measures for Public Libraries* as indicators of public library productivity. Yet the primary value of these measures is as an indicator of the extent to which services successfully attract users. The continued focus on only a few of the many possible outputs of public libraries' services has limited the use and even fostered the misuse of these measures.

The misuse of output measures, such as in the Hennen American Public Library Rating (HAPLR) weighting system, has made it more difficult to see and appreciate the wide range of activities in which libraries engage.[19] The HAPLR compounds an emphasis on circulation by factoring this element into the index at least six times (cost per circulation, collection turnover, circulation per full-time-equivalent hour, circulation per capita, circulation per hour, circulation per visit). Circulation, as a metric, reflects only one aspect of library service and provides librarians only with those efficiency indicators associated with getting books out the door. Librarians who use the HAPLR to evaluate their libraries may unfortunately be tempted to focus their energies in those areas currently emphasized by this index. It is not difficult to imagine a tendency to focus on multiple copies of currently requested materials, especially videos and other materials with short circulation periods, to increase the HAPLR score. In times of reduced budgets especially, these actions could have negative impacts on library services.

Furthermore, the HAPLR index attempts to identify the "best" libraries in the nation. It is unfortunate, therefore, that this tool examines such a narrow spectrum of library services. There is no doubt that some libraries at the top of the HAPLR list are also some of the best in the nation, because they do a variety of things well, but these output measures only capture the impact of circulation and fail to capture the other kinds of contributions these libraries make to their communities.

Output measures can, however, be used to begin to put a face on the differences that the public library makes in its community. A recent Hartford (Conn.) Public Library annual report effectively used output measures to show how the community used various types of community-focused library services. The report indicated that

- 4,000 children use the library's homework centers every month
- the American Place reaches 450 immigrants and refugees each month
- 1,000 people each month attend cultural and educational programs at the library
- family literacy programs reach 2,000 children, parents, and day care providers each month

- community librarians attend more than 600 community meetings each year
- 3,000 small businesses, 1,700 entrepreneurs, and 3,250 job seekers receive library assistance each year.[20]

In addition, public libraries have begun to take the additional step of developing metaphors that compare library output to more accessible points of reference. Patton explains: "What . . . statistics cannot do . . . is show the human faces behind the numbers. [It] is important to provide critical context when interpreting statistical outcomes as well as to make sure that the numbers can be understood as representing meaningful changes in the lives of real people."[21] Public library annual reports have begun to incorporate stories of how real people use and benefit from public library services.

Stories and Testimonials: Outcome Indicators

While output measures provide a glimmer as to what the user-centered impacts might be, by themselves they do not reveal the real differences that the library makes in the lives of citizens. That requires focusing specifically on the differences that these encounters with the library make in the lives of the people who use library services. For example, a Boulder (Colo.) Public Library annual report recently featured this item in its "Highlights and Features":

> Our adult literacy program, BoulderReads!, published a book written by a successful adult learner, Janet Driscoll Turner. Titled *Through the Back Door: Memoirs of a Sharecropper's Daughter Who Learned to Read as a Great-Grandmother*, the book earned significant recognition for the literacy program and for Turner, who was featured in regional newspapers and at clubs and fraternal organizations along the Front Range.[22]

A recent annual report of the Providence Public Library began with the following story, titled "Margarita and Vanesa Zuleta: Nurturing a Passion for Reading," complete with a picture of mother and daughter (figure 1-1). This feature is reproduced here in its entirety.

> "The butterfly and the moon were very good friends. They live next to the library. They like to visit the library. La mariposa y la luna son muy buenas amigas. Ellas viven al lado de la biblioteca. A ellas les gusta vistar la biblioteca." This is the award-winning tale by young, bilingual author Vanesa Zuleta, a frequent visitor of the Providence Public Library.

This colorful tale—illustrated in 24-pack Crayola fashion—won the hearts of the judging panel and brought home the bigger message that the Library is a fun and engaging place to learn. Seven-year-old Vanesa, daughter of Margarita Rivera-Zuleta, is beginning to understand what a valued resource the Library can be. To the Zuleta family, library books and library programs have been bringing adventure and opportunity for some time.

"I used to visit the library branches when Vanesa was very young and bring her home books to read," Margarita

Figure 1-1 Showing How Reading Makes a Difference

Courtesy of Providence Public Library

said. Then came a son, David, now four. "Now, I try to take advantage of all the wonderful programs the Library offers," she said.

For Margarita, these opportunities are particularly important. She was born in Puerto Rico and says access to books, as a child, was quite rare. "When I grew up, we were poor," she said. "We didn't have a library. To read was something big."

At the tender age of 14, she and her sister were sent to America, "just to get a better education." She said she relied on the libraries here to help her in school with her projects. Now, a graduate of Worcester State College in psychology, she has a full appreciation of and is an active supporter of literacy.

"When I visited the Providence branches, I discovered children's books written in both Spanish and English. That's when I began picking up information on other programs they offered for children," she said. Vanesa was about four years old when she entered Cradle to Crayons. The parent/child introduction to reading program is one that Vanesa's younger brother now enjoys.

Vanesa has progressed through Cradle to Crayons, Off to a Good Start, and Creating Readers and also has found great enjoyment in the Cuentos Bilingues and Dia de los Ninos, Dia de los Libros programs. She is especially fond of the Cuentos Bilingues program because "she hears English and Spanish, she reads books, plays games and talks with other children in both languages," Margarita said.

"Reading is very important. It will make her (Vanesa) a better person." As Vanesa wrote, "You can learn a lot from reading. Aprendes muchas cosas cuando lees . . . The library is a fun place to go. La biblioteca es un lugar divertido para visitar."[23]

This story, which was a major component of the Providence Public Library's annual report, speaks powerfully about the ways in which the library has enriched the life of one family. It puts a human face on how library services make a difference. While this is only a single story, the annual report suggests that it was chosen because it represents one of the ways that this particular library helps immigrants. The testimonial suggests a variety of outcomes, including, but not limited to, strengthening the family, fostering cultural pride, development of learning skills such as bilingualism, and gains in writing skills. This story does not stand in isolation; it represents the kinds of *outcomes* that result from the library's programs.

When multiplied by a number of families, stories like this one leave the realm of the anecdote and become patterns that indicate the impact that a program has on its participants. This book shows librarians how stories, testimonials, and user feedback can be used as outcome indicators. More important, this book shows how to design and carry out a study that will both reveal the positive outcomes and give clear examples of how a program is not meeting its intended goals—from the perspective of the user.

NOTES

1. J. Preer, "Where Are Libraries in *Bowling Alone?*" discussion of *Bowling Alone: The Collapse and Revival of American Community,* by Robert D. Putnam, *American Libraries* 32, no. 8 (2001): 60–62.
2. Preer, "Where Are Libraries?" 62.
3. Putnam later discussed the role of libraries in building community—specifically the neighborhood effects of the Chicago Public Library system. See Robert D. Putnam, Lewis M. Feldstein, and Don Cohen, *Better Together: Restoring the American Community* (New York: Simon and Schuster, 2003).
4. Preer, "Where Are Libraries?" 62.
5. Institute of Museum and Library Services, *Perspectives on Outcome Based Evaluation for Libraries and Museums* (Washington, D.C.: Institute of Museum and Library Services, 2000), available at http://www.imls.gov/pubs/pdf/pubobe.pdf.
6. J. C. Durrance and K. E. Fisher-Pettigrew, "Toward Developing Measures of the Impact of Library and Information Services," *Reference and User Services Quarterly* 42, no. 1 (2002): 43–53.
7. Institute of Museum and Library Services, *New Directives, New Directions: Documenting Outcomes in IMLS Grants to Libraries and Museums* (Washington, D.C.: Institute of Museum and Library Services, 2001), available at http://www.imls.gov/grants/current/crnt_obebasics.htm.
8. Institute of Museum and Library Services, *Perspectives on Outcome Based Evaluation.*
9. Institute of Museum and Library Services, *New Directives.*
10. Providence Public Library, "Annual Report 2001," http://www.provlib.org/about/report/fpsuccess.htm.
11. Evanston Public Library, "Mission Statement" (October 18, 2000), http://www.evanston.lib.il.us/library/mission-statement.html.

12. Boulder Public Library, "1999 Annual Report," "Mission Statement" section, http://www.boulder.lib.co.us/general/annual/1999/mission.html.
13. S. Nelson, *The New Planning for Results: A Streamlined Approach* (Chicago: American Library Association, 2001).
14. L. K. Wallace, *Libraries, Mission, and Marketing: Writing Mission Statements That Work* (Chicago: American Library Association, 2003).
15. Nelson, *New Planning for Results.*
16. N. A. Van House et al., *Output Measures for Public Libraries*, 2nd ed. (Chicago: American Library Association, 1987).
17. Nelson, *New Planning for Results.*
18. Van House et al., *Output Measures for Public Libraries.*
19. T. Hennen, "Great American Public Libraries: The 2003 HAPLR Rankings," *American Libraries* 34, no. 9 (2003): 44–48.
20. Hartford Public Library, "President's Report," http://www.hartfordpl.lib.ct.us/Presiden01_02.pdf.
21. M. Q. Patton, *Qualitative Research and Evaluation Methods*, 3rd ed. (Thousand Oaks, Calif.: Sage, 2001).
22. Boulder Public Library, "2001 Annual Report," "Recognition and Highlights" section, http://www.boulder.lib.co.us/general/annual/2001/highlights.html.
23. Providence Public Library, "Annual Report 2001," "A Family Place Success Story!" section, http://www.provlib.org/about/report/fpsuccess.htm.

Chapter 2

Outcomes

An Approach That Shows
the Value of Libraries

A Celebration of Outcomes

Several testimonials foreshadowing outcomes were introduced in chapter 1. We know these stories resonate with many librarians who also have stories to tell but lack the tools needed to incorporate these stories into formal outcome studies. Thus such testimonials remain largely part of library lore and have not been effectively used in telling the library story. Moreover, libraries operate in the larger community where all sorts of organizations are now struggling to tell their stories and document their value. This chapter shows how libraries and other organizations have begun to document their value and gather critical feedback from the perspective of their users.

Recently, the Peninsula Partnership Council of San Mateo County, California, hosted its Community Recognition and Awards Celebration to "honor exemplary efforts" of selected community organizations "on behalf of children, youth, and families in San Mateo County." Marian Wright Edelman, founder and president of the Children's Defense Fund, presented the keynote address for the event. Award winners included a variety of community institutions—the Boys and Girls Club, the Legal Aid Society, and the Center for Domestic Violence Prevention, among others—that had made "significant achievements" toward "agreed-upon outcomes for children and youth" in the county. These outcomes ranged from "Children Are Safe" and "Children Are Healthy" to "Children Are Nurtured in a Stable, Caring Environment" and "Children Are out of Trouble."[1]

Two libraries were among the Gold Award winners, honored by their community for the impacts they had made on the lives of children and youth. The Community Learning Center of the South San Francisco Public Library was recognized for its contributions toward "Children Are Succeeding in School"; and the San Mateo County Library's Youth Services Division was there for its efforts in providing "Systems (That) Support Children."[2] In sharing the limelight of this event, these two libraries stood shoulder to shoulder with other community organizations for delivering activities that have real results — outcomes. In the words of IMLS, they had provided "benefits to people as a result of programs and services: specifically, achievements or changes in skill, knowledge, attitude, behavior, condition, or life status for program participants."[3]

The Multitude of Potential Impacts

The contributions of community organizations to the quality of life for the nation's children are likely to continue to be an outcomes focus. Further, communities and even states are increasingly working together to achieve these outcomes and more, spurred on by the federal government's emphasis on accountability. The spectrum of target outcomes includes improved literacy and technology skills, enhanced safety, job readiness, and increased connections to the community. Outcomes reflect changes that occur in people and in organizations; in aggregate, outcomes reflect an organization's or institution's contributions to improving the quality of life in a community.

Figure 2-1, consisting of data from the Making Connections program of the Annie E. Casey Foundation, identifies the kinds of changes — outcomes — that may occur as a result of participating in a program.[4] The categories used are very broad. They range from seemingly small changes that can occur, such as an immigrant discovering an English as a Second Language (ESL) program in the local public library and gradually learning to trust the staff, to a major change such as gaining the language skills necessary to pass the citizenship exam as a result of participation in the program. While not all these categories are to be seen in libraries, it is not too much of an intellectual stretch to see their application to a multiplicity of user-focused library services.

For libraries, outcomes remain an emerging concept, one largely driven by the federal government, but for an increasing number of community and national groups like the United Way, outcomes are becoming an effective way to assess their value to their communities. Indeed, nationwide, program performance and results-based planning, budgeting, and public reporting are becoming the norm.

Figure 2-1   Categories of Outcomes Compiled by the Annie E. Casey Foundation

Outcome Categories	Types of Outcomes: Changes in . . .
Connection to Informal Social Networks	Relationships and interactions among neighbors and families; social, linguistic, and technological isolation; participation in community, religious, or civic activities and organizations; relationships between youth and adults; and neighborhood culture
Connections to Economic Opportunity	Employment, income, assets, debt, and financial services
Building Neighborhood Assets	Neighborhood economy, housing, amenities, nuisances, safety, political power, and resident satisfaction
Family Function	Parental competencies, parenting practices, home safety, and parent child relationships
Child and Family Well-Being	Child health, social adjustment, educational achievement, and economic well-being

Hundreds of agencies in the United States and Canada use outcome evaluation to measure their contributions to communities. Organizations have identified a broad array of benefits to individuals and communities as a result of their interactions with programs.

Outcomes first and foremost accrue to the individual, and thus belong to them. Organizations want to know that immigrants enrolled in community programs, for example, acquire or improve their English language, literacy, or math skills. In the same vein, funders ask agencies to show, for instance, how successful they are in assuring that "people are connected to their communities," a condition that helps communities work more effectively. A typical outcome of another sort may focus on agency contributions to having "parents/guardians acquire/strengthen parenting skills." The United Way tracks both progress in parenting skills and grantees' outcomes for the children—for instance, "young children are prepared to enter kindergarten." The Boys and Girls Clubs of America are similarly interested in monitoring their programs' contributions toward, among other things, youth educational attainment and the development of leadership skills in young people.[5]

Impact, as depicted in the categories in figure 2-1, may also occur at the family and neighborhood levels. In Maryland, a broad array of outcomes is being identified and tracked by the Vital Signs Project of the Baltimore Neighborhood

Indicators Alliance, a collaboration of local citizen action groups, faith-based groups, foundations, and government agencies.[6] The purpose of the project is "to measure our progress toward a shared vision and agreed-upon outcomes for Baltimore neighborhoods over time."[7] It focuses on various aspects of neighborhood improvement, from children and family health, safety, and well-being to workforce and economic development.

Outcomes may be progressive, such that gains made at one level, i.e., the individual, can reverberate across the spectrum of human aggregation, generating benefits for families, neighborhoods, and communities at large. The outcome evaluation of Project Literacy Victoria, prepared for the provincial government of British Columbia in a climate of increasing political transparency and accountability, showed that with initial literacy gains, such as "Learners Gain Basic Reading and Writing Skills," Project Literacy Victoria's adult learners were able to "refine and consolidate skills and begin to use them in daily life."[8] They could

- read, interpret, and use information necessary in their personal lives (e.g., bus schedules, phone books, and recipes)
- read, interpret, and use information necessary at work (e.g., manuals and forms)
- write as necessary for work (e.g., memos, correspondence, and e-mail)
- perform tasks necessary for personal and household management (e.g., write checks and balance checkbooks)
- locate and access community resources (e.g., attend events)
- expand networks and increase participation in the community (e.g., seek advice, encourage others to access literacy services)
- enroll in further education, and more (e.g., enroll in courses, take and pass assessment tests)

Over time, as their outcomes accrued, Project Literacy Victoria learners grew more empowered. Although Project Literacy Victoria could not take full credit for long-term outcomes for learners, they "believe that (the) program influenced them in a non-trivial way." Learners began "to be able to live independently," "become more employable," and "communicate better within their families and with their children's schools." Given the sheer breadth of outcomes captured by the evaluation of a single literacy effort in Victoria, British Columbia, it comes as no surprise that program evaluators determined that a "one size fits all" assessment approach would not have worked.[9] We argue that these same types of outcomes accrue to participants in adult-learning programs in libraries.

The "How Libraries and Librarians Help" Outcome Model

Through a generous grant from the Institute of Museum and Library Services, the authors recently completed a research study entitled "How Libraries and Librarians Help: Context-Centered Methods for Evaluating Public Library Efforts at Bridging the Digital Divide and Building Community." The study was conducted by a team of researchers from the University of Michigan and the University of Washington to identify from best-practice examples how libraries and librarians make a difference. This research, using qualitative approaches, empirically examined the *use* of specific community-focused services to develop context-sensitive approaches and instruments that identify outcomes. The services studied included those designed for immigrant populations, after-school community technology programs for teens, community networks, information and referral services, programs designed around ethnicity, and consumer health information services. Aggregating the results, figure 2-2 shows the types of outcomes experienced by participants in the programs we studied.

Figure 2-2   Selected List of Candidate Public Library Outcomes
Identified by "How Libraries and Librarians Help"

- Attitude changes (e.g., negative to positive)
- Increased ability to access information
- Personal efficacy (self-esteem, confidence building, a changed outlook on life and future prospects, feelings of accomplishment and hope)
- Skill levels increased (e.g., increased technological literacy, language facility, communication skills, social skills, etc.)
- Learning gains (e.g., increased interest in learning, active participation in learning, etc.)
- Knowledge gains (wide range, individually focused, e.g., knowledge of the community, knowledge needed to pass the GED, etc.)
- Progress toward a goal
- Social networks (e.g., increased social and community connections, increased social capital)
- Status changes (e.g., decide to return to school, get a job, become a citizen, increased participation as a citizen)
- Decreased transaction "costs" (saving time, money, and energy, increased convenience)

These outcome categories and the subcategories indicated in parentheses were identified from a small group of libraries whose best-practice community-focused services were the basis of a series of user-centered outcomes studies. A series of detailed case studies in part 3 of this book show how these, and other outcomes, emerged.

Libraries Make a Difference

The How Libraries and Librarians Help studies that resulted in the HLLH outcome model presented in this book showed us a variety of ways that libraries contribute to a range of outcomes that are both similar to and different from those of community organizations. IMLS has worked hard to get librarians to think in terms of outcomes, and for good reason. Although the concept of outcome evaluation may be new to the library world, the outcomes themselves—the library's contributions to community—are not. Every day libraries generate the kinds of "benefits to people as a result of programs and services" sought by IMLS. In essence, institutional efficacy is not the problem; the lack of effective communication tools is.

Historically, libraries have measured the scale of their productivity in outputs, often focusing on circulation. We have shown that output measures reflect only one aspect of "the library story." It is time for librarians themselves to benefit from outcomes research, and begin to discover and document what intuition suggests about the power of libraries. Through outcome evaluation, librarians may begin to identify impacts that are the result of the interactions that people have with specific activities that make up targeted library services.

Fortunately, as they embark on this new approach, librarians can turn to their clientele for assistance. As an evaluation approach, outcome evaluation affords participants a mechanism to frame the impact of their interaction with the service in their own words. For libraries, user feedback via focus groups, interviews, and surveys not only serves as a critical frontline barometer of the library's effectiveness; like no other source, it can paint a detailed and sometimes very personal portrait of the depth of impact that libraries have on people's lives. Give a user the chance to speak, and the public librarian gains access to a wealth of information about the results of the user's interaction with the library service and its impacts.

Libraries Help in Many Ways

Like other community organizations, libraries are community-focused institutions that help to make a difference in a variety of ways. From New York to California and Washington, to Texas and Michigan, the public libraries that participated in the How Libraries and Librarians Help study demonstrate the range of benefits that libraries bring to children, individuals, families, and communities at large. The outcome examples below illustrate not only the context of each outcome, they also show the variety of impacts that libraries make in their communities from the perspective of participants.

Participant testimonials, whether brief statements or robustly narrated stories, do furnish the raw material of outcomes, which evaluators can collect and examine for patterns. Patterns of impacts, found participant by participant, comment by comment, story by story, indicate the occurrence of outcomes. The examples below have been taken from several HLLH studies to illustrate some of the supporting evidence we found for specific library outcomes. Under each outcome category in the following section are quotes taken from users and from library staff. Part 3 of this book brings together integrated case studies that show in much more detail how specific libraries and librarians help their communities.

Outcome: Children Have a Safe Place to Go to after School

Activities that foster the library as a safe place. Austin (Tex.) Public Library branches are centrally located in communities and are clean and well-lit. Librarians offer an informal, welcoming environment, and make computers visible; they also "triage" kids coming through the door, recommending appropriate activities and work spaces for them. One user told the research team that until recently, he had waited for his mother at a spot between his school and the public library. A police officer told him that the spot was not a safe place, and suggested other places to wait, including the public library. The student went to the library, and discovered the "Wired for Youth" Center. He now goes to the center most days after school.

Outcome from the perspective of caregivers:

In this one branch that now has eighty kids every day after school, these kids were previously hanging out on the streets after school.

I knew [name of staff member]. I am very leery about what adults I have my child around. She's not flaky or airy. I am comfortable with [name of staff member]'s personality.

Outcome: Teens Build Technology, Communication, and Outreach Skills

Activities that foster development of teens' skills. The Flint (Mich.) Public Library sponsors the Community Information Agents Online (CIAO) program to teach local teens technology skills and provide them with the knowledge they need to become more active in their community. Library staff offer current technology and hands-on instruction, encourage teens' self-expression, and support social networks.

Outcome from the perspective of teens:

[Before CIAO when] speaking to people, I was more kind of an antisocial person. When I first started, I really didn't talk to people I don't know well. I'd have to completely just know you for so long before I'd talk to you. Now I can talk to almost anybody about anything no matter where I am.

So, learning how to work with web pages and work on the Internet and then working with the different community organizations, it has helped me not just with the computers, but it has helped me get involved more than I was in my community.

Outcome: Immigrants Bridge Cultural Landscapes— the Old and the New

Activities that help immigrants to bridge cultural landscapes. In addition to multi-lingual collection development, the Queens (N.Y.) Public Library provides computers with which to e-mail friends and family back home, sponsors cultural arts programming to celebrate diversity, and offers free access to information and citizenship classes to facilitate immigrants' transition to American life.

Outcome from perspective of immigrants:

There are computers for use by the public, this is really important . . . I will use the computers to keep in touch with my friends who are in Peru.

I came with my daughter to see a Korean music and dance performance . . . I want my daughter to appreciate her native culture and this was an excellent opportunity for her to watch and learn.

The black history month activities can certainly help me to know more about African culture and music.

I feel I am more American by using the library.

Outcome: Human Services Providers Feel Empowered by Increased Connections among Agencies

Activities that foster service providers' empowerment. Community Information Program (CIP) staff in San Mateo County, California, connect service providers and agencies through database and publication services, as well as through regular CIP-sponsored orientations and meetings located throughout the county.

Outcome from perspective of service providers:

I can connect with other organizations (through CIP publications).

We've talked; we know who we are. It's very, very helpful to have that personal contact at the provider meetings . . . at the CIP orientation and you will also meet key people in the field of social services and nonprofit organizations. So, this is a must; and people come back saying wow!

The Multiple Benefits of Outcome Evaluation

Since the inception of its outcome evaluation program, hundreds of volunteers and staff of local United Ways in the United States and Canada have attended outcome evaluation training sessions (as have members of health, human services, and youth-serving organizations from across the country) to increase their effectiveness as well as learn to document what differences local organizations are making in their communities.[10] The outcome evaluation process generates helpful outcomes of its own. Community organizations gain knowledge with which to demonstrate their accountability and augment their efficacy (through improved decision making, resource allocation, and program and service improvements), and they receive a valuable infusion of marketing information with which to broadcast the impact of their services to their community, their funders, and their government. According to a United Way survey of agencies that had adopted outcome measurement approaches:

> Respondents agreed that implementing program outcome measurement was helpful, particularly in the areas of communicating program results (88%), focusing staff effort on common goals and purposes (88%), clarifying the purpose of the program (86%), identifying effective practices (84%), and successfully competing for resources funding (83%). In addition, there was agreement on its helpfulness in enhancing record-keeping systems (80%), and improving the service delivery of the program (76%).[11]

These responses point to many of the proven advantages of outcome evaluation. By discovering and documenting their services' impact, community-based organizations not only gain insight for themselves and their funders into what they do well (and what they do poorly), but also how they can do things better.

The work of Peter Hernon and his colleagues on service quality adds to the library field's knowledge of outcomes, particularly those resulting from academic library services.[12] The "Counting on Results" study comprised a multistage research design that asked a broad range of librarians to identify possible outcomes that were then tested by users.[13] Researchers of information behavior are also studying the outcomes of children's use of information technologies in public libraries.[14] The need for assistance with evaluating community program use was clearly voiced in our recent survey of library professionals: 73 percent said their current evaluation tools were inadequate for assessing the impact of their services on individuals, families, and communities.[15]

In her introduction to *Perspectives on Outcome Based Evaluation for Libraries and Museums,* Beverly Sheppard of the Institute of Museum and Library Services underscores the range of benefits that libraries can expect from outcome evaluation:

> [Outcome evaluation] helps . . . institutions identify their successes and share their stories with a wide range of stakeholders . . . Evaluation provides the critical feedback that tells what is working, what must be changed, and how a program may be improved. It helps inform difficult decisions. Realigning staff or reallocating financial resources are far more palatable when supported by evidence that these investments are making a difference. Well-designed evaluation further enables advocacy and partnership. Good stories become convincing and forge the basis for ongoing funding support and collaboration.[16]

Peggy Rudd concurs.[17] For her, outcomes can be a powerful tool with which to

- communicate program and service benefits to the community
- demonstrate accountability and justify funding needs to funders and resource allocators
- build partnerships and promote community collaborations
- determine which programs and services should be expanded or replicated
- identify exemplary programs and services for recognition

As librarians initiate more assessments and evaluations to document the impact they have on their communities, they will be able to take advantage of the benefits outlined in this chapter and stake their claim in a national discourse already well under way. Librarians will be able to speak a common language with other agencies about their contributions to civic engagement and community life and to articulate to key audiences, like never before, the vital and unique role that public libraries play in civil society.

Knowing outcomes, librarians will find themselves empowered to improve strategic planning and finally narrate "the library story." They will be better able to equip themselves to compete for scarce dollars. By infusing marketing vehicles like presentations, reports, newsletters, flyers, and bond issue campaigns with evidence of their services' impact, librarians will send strong, consistent messages of their value proposition for their communities. In publicizing positive outcomes we also place emphasis on identifying negative outcomes, which provide invaluable feedback for improving existing services and initiating new ones.

Such is the powerful potential not only of marketing with outcomes, but of branding with them—in this case, enhancing the public library's community brand, one indelible enough to induce stakeholders to include libraries in studies of societal institutions and social capital and in major government and foundation initiatives. We thereby showcase libraries as frontline anchors, even primary engines, of our democratic society. Indeed, as articulated in their mission statements, public libraries support Thomas Jefferson's charge for an "enlightened citizenry [that] is indispensable for the proper functioning of a republic." Libraries not only help enlighten the citizenry (and those who wish to become citizens); they can, as we have discovered and documented in our exploration of outcomes, engage, enhance, and empower people in myriad ways.

NOTES

1. County of San Mateo, *Children in Our Community: A Report on Their Health and Well-Being* (Redwood City, Calif.: Harbor, 2000), available at http://www.plsinfo.org/healthysmc/33/children.pdf.
2. County of San Mateo, *Children in Our Community*.
3. Institute of Museum and Library Services, *New Directives, New Directions: Documenting Outcomes in IMLS Grants to Libraries and Museums* (Washington, D.C.: Institute of Museum and Library Services, 2001), available at http://www.imls.gov/grants/current/crnt_obebasics.htm.
4. Annie E. Casey Foundation, "Making Connections: National Survey Indicators Database," http://www.aecf.org/initiatives/mc/mcid/index.php.
5. Boys and Girls Clubs of Greater Washington, "Specific Program Outcomes," http://www.bgcgw.org/what/outcomes.html.
6. Baltimore Neighborhood Indicators Alliance, "Baltimore's Neighborhood Vital Signs," http://www.bnia.org/vitalsigns/index.html.
7. Baltimore Neighborhood Indicators Alliance, "Neighborhood News Flash" (2002), http://www.charm.net/~cheswolde/cheswolde/Flash/flash_112202.htm.
8. Project Literacy Victoria, *Outcome Measurement for a Community Literacy Program* (Victoria, B.C.: Project Literacy Victoria, 2001), available at http://www.plv.bc.ca/outcome/cover.htm.
9. Project Literacy Victoria, *Outcome Measurement*.

10. United Way of America, *Outcome Measurement Resource Network—Who Is Involved in Outcome Measurement?* (Alexandria, Va.: United Way of America, 2002), available at http://national.unitedway.org/outcomes/initiatives/national.cfm.
11. United Way of America, *Outcome Measurement: What and Why, an Overview* (Alexandria, Va.: United Way of America, 2002), available at http://national.unitedway.org/outcomes/files/TPsOMWhatandWhy.pdf.
12. P. Hernon and E. Altman, *Service Quality in Academic Libraries* (Norwood, N.J.: Ablex, 1996); P. Hernon and E. Altman, *Assessing Service Quality: Satisfying the Expectations of Library Customers* (Chicago: American Library Association, 1998); P. Hernon and R. E. Dugan, *An Action Plan for Outcomes Assessment in Your Library* (Chicago: American Library Association, 2002); P. Hernon and D. Nitecki, "Service Quality: A Concept Not Fully Explored," *Library Trends* 49, no. 4 (2001): 687–708.
13. K. C. Lance et al., *Counting on Results: New Tools for Outcome-Based Evaluation of Public Libraries: Final Report* (Washington, D.C.: Institute of Museum and Library Services, 2002); N. Steffen, K. C. Lance, and R. Logan, "Time to Tell the Whole Story: Outcome-Based Evaluation and the Counting on Results Project," *Public Libraries* 41 (2002): 222–28; N. Steffen and K. C. Lance, "Who's Doing What: Outcome-Based Evaluation and Demographics in the Counting on Results Project," *Public Libraries* 41 (2002): 271–79.
14. E. T. Dresang, M. Gross, and L. E. Holt, "Project CATE: Using Outcome Measures to Assess School-Age Children's Use of Technology in Urban Public Libraries: A Collaborative Research Process," *Library and Information Science Research* 25, no. 1 (2003): 19–42.
15. J. C. Durrance and K. E. Pettigrew, "Community Information: The Technological Touch," *Library Journal* 125, no. 2 (2000): 44–46.
16. Institute of Museum and Library Services, *Perspectives on Outcome Based Evaluation for Libraries and Museums* (Washington, D.C.: Institute of Museum and Library Services, 2000), available at http://www.imls.gov/pubs/pdf/pubobe.pdf.
17. Institute of Museum and Library Services, *Perspectives on Outcome Based Evaluation.*

Chapter 3

The "How Libraries and Librarians Help" Outcome Model

*Applying Contextual Approaches
to Outcome Evaluation*

The How Libraries and Librarians Help (HLLH) outcome evaluation model owes much to approaches to outcome assessment that have emerged in the social services and nonprofit sectors. In the past few years several outcome models have emerged (e.g., United Way, 2002; W. K. Kellogg Foundation, 2001).[1] Models such as the United Way Program outcome model (discussed below) generally focus on four components: inputs, activities, outputs, and the culminating component—outcomes. (See figure 3-1.)

Figure 3-1 The United Way Outcome Model

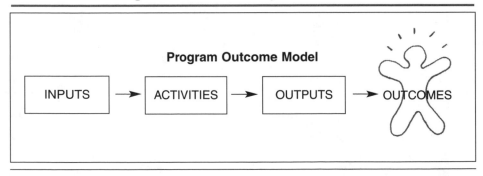

Program Outcome Model

INPUTS → ACTIVITIES → OUTPUTS → OUTCOMES

The HLLH model also incorporates four types of factors essential to the effective assessment of service outcomes: the library service model, the users, relevant service outputs, and, finally, the outcomes themselves. These factors are outlined below.

The first set of factors is associated with the *library service* model, including the specific activities that the user interacts with as well as the essential role that staff play in shaping the program.

The second set of factors concerns the people who need to interact with a service—the *users* or clientele.

The third set includes the traditional *outputs* component that appears in most outcome models today.

The final set of factors consists of the *outcomes* that result from users' interactions with the specific service activities.

Figure 3-2 shows the relationships among these factors.

Figure 3-2   The "How Libraries and Librarians Help" Outcome Model

Contextual Factors Associated with the Institution	Contextual Factors Associated with Users	Outputs	Outcomes
The library and the library service model Strategies and approaches; specific activities undertaken Professional contributions from staff Other inputs and resources used to carry out the program	Needs, attitudes, and perceptions Information behavior Approaches, limitations, and factors that affect interaction with the program	The numbers of clients who are served In various ways. "How much is done for how many people?"	The changes in people's lives; "benefits to people: specifically, achievements or changes in skill, knowledge, attitude, behavior, condition, or life status"

The HLLH Model: A Detailed Overview

The HLLH outcome model shows that outcomes result from specific factors in combination. The strength (or weakness) of an outcome thus depends on the relative strengths (or weaknesses) of its contextual components. This model asks librarians to examine the factors associated with the library's service model itself, because service model factors reflect both the library's philosophy of service and its ability to deliver needed services. In other models, a variety of contextual factors is assumed to be included under the heading of "inputs." This model makes these contextual factors explicit.

The HLLH outcome model has been influenced by (1) information behavior research, which has produced a large body of knowledge that helps to explain the complexity of information seeking and use;[2] and (2) several research projects that have focused on identifying outcomes from best-practice libraries.[3] Each of the outcome model components is discussed below with examples from best-practice libraries.

Contextual Factors Associated with the Institution

Library service factors are covered in most other outcome models simply as "inputs," which implies only resources that go into the particular service. The HLLH outcome model starts (like most other models) with inputs, which provide the lifeblood of the service, but includes, in addition to the nature of the service, the specific activities that make up the particular service, and the contributions of the staff. Thus in the HLLH model this factor is not referred to simply as inputs, but as institutional factors.

Users understand the library through their interactions with the specific activities that together make up the service. Activities, as we will see in the discussion of outputs below, are the parents of outputs. Activities vary considerably and in libraries have been undercounted, with the exception of the overcounted activities associated with circulation. Outcome evaluation will assist staff in identifying and counting activities, incorporating them into outputs, and, finally, showing how activities contribute to outcomes.

Staff members are also crucial to the institutional component. It is difficult to overestimate the contributions of the staff to achieving successful outcomes. By providing examples from best practice, this book will show how the library staff shape outcomes. Staff frame the service model, recruit the clientele, and develop the activities that lead to outcomes. Staff in the libraries we examined shared the following characteristics: they were committed to their clientele, creative in their approach to providing service, entrepreneurial in their approaches to seeking additional resources, and were able to articulate some, though not all, of the outcomes of their services. Some of them had been recruited to their jobs specifically because of special skills that they brought to the service, such as language facility, interest in the clientele, ability to teach, or knowledge of information technology. Library staff made many contributions to significant outcomes, often starting by changing the perceptions that teen or adult users brought with them to a service; misperceptions about library services limit a person's ability to obtain the full range of benefits from a particular program.

The HLLH outcome model helps library staff identify the service activities that lead to the outputs and outcomes. The case study examples provided in part 3 of this book show the creativity of the staff in designing activities targeted to a specific group of users. They also show that outcomes can help librarians gain a rich knowledge of how they help their users.

Contextual Factors Associated with the User

Outcome-focused evaluation has users at its center. Outcomes accrue to individuals, groups, and communities. Program participants are, of course, any outcome study's primary informants. An important focus of the HLLH outcome model is the specific articulation of the needs, attitudes, and perceptions that users bring to their participation in a program. Users come with various strengths and limitations, varying needs and interests, etc. All these factors affect their interaction with the program. The individuals who participate in community-focused programs of various kinds vary considerably; this is true even of participants in the same program. This book helps librarians factor the user into outcome assessment of a particular service. Because of the strengths and limitations that users bring to a particular service, the outcomes for particular individuals will not be identical. Therefore outcome evaluation needs to look for basic changes in the individual, as well as high-end outcomes.

In the same vein, this book helps librarians look not only for obvious outcomes but also for unexpected or unintended outcomes as well as negative ones, which can be used to improve current services and design new ones. For example, teens in community technology programs came in order to gain technology skills and left with considerably more, gaining skills of working with others, increased self-confidence, and increased participation in the community. Often, however, they indicated that they needed to overcome negative perceptions of librarians and begin to trust them before they were able to reap the benefits of the programs in which they participated.

Outputs: "How Much Is Done for How Many People?"

The set of outputs developed for librarians in the 1980s has long since outlived its usefulness.[4] In recent years library administrators and service developers have begun to develop more creative approaches to presenting library outputs. Output data, if properly selected, can act as a strong contributor to understanding and presenting outcomes. The kinds of outputs that can contribute to meaningful outcome assessment are those that present an accounting of the use of a variety of activities designed to meet the needs of a particular group of people. Thus, outputs can be measured as the number of people who attend such activities as ESL tutoring classes, workshops on various topics such as e-mail for beginners or computer literacy for seniors, or collaboratively developed programs on medical topics; these produce outputs that focus on the numbers of people who attended or participated in these activities.

Staff of the Queens (N.Y.) Borough Public Library, for example, have developed a set of activities for immigrants that together make up the New Americans Program. These activities comprise hundreds of public programs per year on multiple topics, including cultural programs, etc.; English for Speakers of Other Languages (ESOL) classes at various levels; tutoring; conversation groups; workshops on coping skills of various sorts; collaboration with community organizations; and extensive marketing using ethnic media.

These programs and classes are attended by thousands of individuals; these visits are counted as outputs. Users of the Queens library's New Americans Program are likely to interact with only a few of these activities. The program's outcomes accrue to the thousands of individuals who participate in a myriad array of activities. What outcomes accrue to which individuals depends on the nature of the interaction with a specific set of activities. Outcome identification will be discussed in the next section.

Outcomes: Putting It All Together

Continuing with the immigrant example, outcomes must be measured from the perspective of the user. Many immigrants who interact with the services of the New Americans Program gain skills in reading and speaking English; they are also likely to gain confidence in themselves and their ability to maneuver in their new country. A number of unexpected outcomes might also be found if one looks carefully. Outcomes for immigrants begin with learning how to exploit an important community resource (the library)—a very important gain for people who may not have experienced a public library before coming to the United States. Until the immigrant discovers the public library, other outcomes cannot occur. After accruing these basic building-block gains, immigrants may then experience a wide range of personal gains, including increased self-confidence and various skills in using information technology (such as interactive literacy software), and they may make gains for their families, build social networks, or become better prepared for employment.

Program outcomes, as we will show throughout this book, can be grouped into sets of patterns that result from the particular program context and the types of interactions that people make with the program. Figure 3-3, titled "Ripples of Impact of a Basic Literacy Program," shows groups of outcomes that resulted from the well-established Washtenaw Literacy program housed in the Ypsilanti District Library in Michigan.[5]

The outcomes experienced by learners in the Washtenaw Literacy program are numerous and broad in range, extending beyond basic literacy and impacting just about every aspect of learners' lives. The program touches not only the lives of learners but reaches into the lives of those around them—in their families, at their workplaces, and in the larger community. A conceptual model for observed outcome patterns can be viewed in figure 3-3. This graphic is the result of group-

Figure 3-3   Ripples of Impact of a Basic Literacy Program

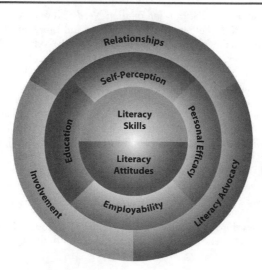

ing outcomes into categories, and represents a progression of outcomes starting with learners' direct literacy benefits and moving outward into outcomes in key areas of personal change enabled by improved literacy. At the outer edge of the ripple are outcome categories extending beyond the learner to impact his or her relationships and environment.

This chapter identified the components of the HLLH outcome model. In part 2 of this book we present the four steps of the How Libraries and Librarians Help outcome model. These steps can by used by librarians to determine the outcomes of a variety of library services. The strength of the HLLH model is the creation of a simple yet flexible approach to identifying the relevant factors that contribute to a specific library's set of outcomes. The result of using this approach is the creation of a set of relevant outcomes that grow from the service model and that incorporate the needs of library users.

NOTES

1. United Way of America, *Outcome Measurement Resource Network—Who Is Involved in Outcome Measurement?* (Alexandria, Va.: United Way of America, 2002), available at http://national.unitedway.org/outcomes/initiatives/national.cfm; W. K. Kellogg Foundation, *Logic Model Development Guide* (Battle Creek, Mich.: W. K. Kellogg Foundation, 2001), available at http://www.wkkf.org/ Pubs/Tools/Evaluation/Pub3669.pdf.

2. D. O. Case, *Looking for Information: A Survey of Research on Information Seeking, Needs, and Behavior* (Amsterdam, Neth.: Academic Press, 2002).

3. J. C. Durrance et al., *Serving Job Seekers and Career Changers: A Planning Manual for Public Libraries* (Chicago: Public Library Association, 1993); J. C. Durrance, *Armed for Action: Library Response to Citizen Information Needs* (New York: Neal-Schuman, 1994); J. C. Durrance and K. E. Pettigrew, "How Libraries and Librarians Help: Toward Context-Centered Methods for Evaluating Public Library Networked Community Information Initiatives," *First Monday* 6, no. 4 (April 2001), http://firstmonday.org/ issues/issue6_4/durrance/index.html; J. C. Durrance and K. E. Pettigrew, *Online Community Information: Creating a Nexus at Your Library* (Chicago: American Library Association, 2002); K. E. Fisher, J. C. Durrance, and M. B. Hinton, "Information Grounds and the Use of Need-Based Services by Immigrants in Queens, NY: A Context-Based, Outcome Evaluation Approach," *Journal of the American Society for Information Science and Technology* 55, no. 8 (2004): 754–66; K. E. Pettigrew, J. C. Durrance, and K. T. Unruh, "Facilitating Community Information-Seeking Using the Internet: Findings from Three Public Library-Community Network Systems," *Journal of the American Society for Information Science and Technology* 53, no. 11 (2002): 894–903.

4. N. A. Van House et al., *Output Measures for Public Libraries*, 2nd ed. (Chicago: American Library Association, 1987).

5. This figure was developed by Maria Souden and Sarah Wooden. It also appears as part of their study of the Washtenaw Literacy program in part 3 of this book.

Part II

How to Measure and Predict the Outcomes of Your Own Library Programs and Services

Step One

*Getting Started: Preparing to Conduct
an Outcomes Study*

In part 1 we introduced outcomes and explained why it is essential for librarians to consider the contributions of the library service model and the activities and staff used to carry out a specific service—such as the Queens Borough Public Library's New Americans Program—in order to identify and measure outcomes. In short, programs vary considerably, and you want to determine the outcomes of *your* program. Because no two programs are alike, you need to examine carefully what you put into the program—the set of activities that have been designed for a specific set of users, not to mention resources and staffing. You also, of course, need to examine the users who interact with specific aspects of the service (while thinking of those who don't but could benefit). Outcomes result from the influence of a specific program on its users.

Our studies show that often librarians have hunches about the differences that their services make, i.e., the outcomes. However, until now librarians haven't had the tools to help codify these hunches. The exercise in this chapter is designed to focus your attention on the available evidence that suggests service outcomes. (Chapter 8, by Rhea Rubin, can also help librarians who are at the beginning stages of developing a service to anticipate a basic set of outcomes.)

To help librarians determine service outcomes we have devised a four-step process, starting with an initial assessment process that frames the outcome context and continuing through the process of collecting and analyzing data that result in determining specific outcomes, which we explain here in part 2.

However, we don't stop there, nor should you. The most important part of the outcome study process is using what you find in a variety of ways. The third part of the book, chapters 9 through 12, provides numerous examples of specific outcomes. These chapters document the kinds of specifics that jog the memories of various staff members and can help you to tailor the exercise in this chapter to *your* service.

To start the process we have developed an initial exercise, "Preparing to Determine Program Impacts," to help you identify the service that you wish to evaluate, its specific services and users, and its potential positive and negative outcomes *from the perspective of its direct users and other stakeholders.* Consider your responses "rough guesses" or working expectations that you will confirm in the course of your outcomes study.

EXERCISE 4-1
Preparing to Determine Program Impacts

1. Determine the scope of the evaluation study.
   - Which service is to be evaluated?
   - Which activity(s) of the service is to be studied (e.g., ESOL classes for immigrants, tutoring, conversation groups)? Which user group(s) and other stakeholders are to be included in the study?

2. For the activities listed above, potentially who is affected by them? (Think broadly about this, e.g., include families of direct users, etc.)

3. What positive (or negative) outcomes do you think are experienced by these stakeholders as a result of the activities (and may not yet have been able to document)?

Think, for example, about user commentaries as powerful indicators of outcomes. If you can identify them, then you are well on your way to devising an outcome study that reflects your service's impacts, so recount a story or user comment that reflects a service outcome (positive or negative; expected or unexpected) experienced by a user of the library service.

In addition, brainstorm a list of "ideal outcomes" that would help to build the strongest case for the benefits of the service. What differences does this service make in people's lives?

Be explicit about your assumptions of the outcomes that you consider likely to appear via data collection. Your data collection methods (discussed in the next chapter) will elicit likely outcomes, in addition to ferreting out unexpected outcomes—i.e., those of which you are unaware.

The text in figure 4-1 illustrates how we used our approach to evaluate the impact of two programs geared toward new immigrants and sponsored by the Queens Borough Public Library.

Figure 4-1 Potential Program Impacts of the Queens Borough Public Library's New Americans and Adult Learner Programs

Activities to Be Studied	Who Is Potentially Affected?	Possible Positive and Negative Outcomes
English language and literacy classes tailored to meet immigrant student needs at basic, beginning, intermediate, and advanced levels	Immigrant students and their families Immigrant students and their families and friends, local employers	Increased language and communication skills; enhanced job preparedness; families now also use library; library's visibility increased
Coping skills classes designed to help new immigrants learn about and adapt to life in America		More adept at navigating and participating in everyday American life (attend school, gain employment, help children, socialize, preserve culture, etc.)

Chapter 5

Step Two

*Collecting Data for Outcomes:
Approaches and Tools*

Once you have determined the scope and targets of your outcome study, you are well prepared for the next stage of the process: determining your data collection methods and identifying the sensitivities and special needs of particular user groups. As emphasized in the previous chapter, planning is a crucial step in any research process, and particularly so in librarians' first round of outcome determination. Outcome findings must result from strong planning and data collection methods that accurately reflect the activities that the library uses to serve particular client groups.

In this inaugural stage of outcome study for public libraries, the field lacks a variety of established data collection models. Our "Getting Started" chapter helped librarians to enter into the process with ideas of where to look for evidence of outcomes—in the words of people who participate in the programs and services under examination.

In these initial rounds of outcome study, when librarians do not have an outcome history with which to predict the impacts of their programs and services, well-designed tools that target service participants, such as interviews, focus groups, and observation, can effectively harvest the raw material of outcomes: participant behavior and feedback. For librarians who completed initial outcome studies and wish to monitor their outcomes long-term or longitudinally, surveys can be an additional helpful data collection method.

To help you prepare data collection instruments for initial outcome studies, this chapter offers

- at-a-glance descriptions of the different data collection methods that librarians can use and combine

- examples of open-ended questions to ask particular client groups and other stakeholders to determine outcomes

- a preparation exercise for customizing data collection methods and questions to particular users and services

Additional examples of data collection instruments and how they were used are found in part 3 as well as in the Outcomes Toolkit, which is available at our website (http://ibec.ischool.washington.edu/).

Deciding Which Data Collection Approach Is Best

Your data collection methods will depend on the context, the goals of your study, and the resources that are available; bear in mind that different data collection methods can suit particular purposes, and we strongly recommend using them in combination with one another (this is known as "triangulation"). Below we offer detailed summaries for the *primary data collection methods that we recommend for initial studies: focus groups and interviews.* These summaries include definitions, how to's, and comparisons of strengths and weaknesses to help guide your choice of approaches and combinations.

We encourage librarians involved in an initial study to use primary data collection methods such as focus groups and interviews to collect as much detailed data from staff and users as possible. In addition, you may choose to use supplemental approaches, such as observation, follow-up interviews, and surveys, to verify information and to discover richer outcomes as well as to collect data on professional contributions.

One final note: it is crucial when conducting any field study to consider the full context of your research setting. Think carefully about the best ways to collect data from the users of your chosen service. Important questions to consider include: *What logistical challenges are involved? How can we best glean important stories or examples for each outcome? And especially, do certain user groups have particular sensitivities that might affect service outcomes and dictate data collection methods?* When studying new immigrants, for example, you might opt for short, confidential interviews run by someone that the users trust and in the language in which they feel most comfortable.

Primary Data Collection Methods

Focus Groups

FOCUS GROUPS DEFINED

A focus group is in essence a group interview with six to ten people of similar background. Gathering people together to share their thoughts regarding questions and issues about library programs can be an efficient way of collecting substantial data in a single setting.

FOCUS GROUP HOW TO'S

To gather data in a library setting using focus groups, consider the following points.

When conducting a focus group, which typically lasts one to two hours, we recommend a minimum of two persons serving as facilitators: one person to lead the discussion, and one person to take notes on the content of the conversations, as well as the nonverbal communication that devices such as a tape recorder cannot capture. Noting nonverbal behavior such as nods of approval (or disapproval) and facial and body expressions of interest (or lack thereof) can provide additional meaning to the flow of conversation during the focus group.

Our research team frequently used both focus groups and interviews when evaluating community and library programs. In a focus group setting, for example, service providers can absorb what similar professionals are experiencing. Such opportunities often nurture members' thoughts that may not have occurred to them had they participated in a one-on-one interview. During a personal interview, the experiences that participants share are typically on a more personal level, and therefore the dynamics of a one-on-one interview often provide for richer data collection. (See the "Interviews" section of this chapter for more details on using this data collection method.)

Ensure that your focus group occurs at times and in a venue that is convenient for participants, but outside the evaluated service setting, i.e., the library, to minimize biased responses known as the Hawthorne Effect (when participants give responses that they believe the investigators desire). Also, be sure to provide beverages and snacks—never underestimate the importance of food for stimulating participation and social interaction!

FOCUS GROUP STRENGTHS

- Excellent approach to gather in-depth attitudes and beliefs from several stakeholders at a time
- Group dynamics might generate more ideas than individual interviews

- Can be effectively used to focus on details regarding issues found through surveys or other data collection methods

FOCUS GROUP WEAKNESSES

- Requires staff time to set up and facilitate focus group
- Requires staff time to identify and schedule participants for focus group
- Requires strong facilitator to guide discussion and ensure participation by all members
- Usually requires special equipment to record and transcribe focus group discussion

We conducted several focus groups with teenage participants in the Wired for Youth (WFY) program—an after-school drop-in program aimed at providing computers to youth in or near low-income areas in selected branches of the Austin (Tex.) Public Library. The "Focus Group Guide" that we used appears below. As with all our instruments, this guide begins with a scope note, which explains the purpose of the instrument.

WFY Youth Participant Focus Group Guide

Scope Note: This protocol was used for focus groups made up of youth who frequently visit the "Wired for Youth" centers. The youth librarians helped us identify and recruit students to participate in the focus groups prior to our research visit to Austin. The librarians also helped us obtain parental consent prior to the focus groups.

INTRODUCTION

Explain why we're here.

Can everyone tell us your name and how old you are and why you come to Wired for Youth?

Where else do you use computers? How is this different?

HOW WIRED FOR YOUTH WORKS

What did you do this week at Wired for Youth?

What do you usually do at Wired for Youth?

How does Wired for Youth work?

What do the librarians do as part of Wired for Youth?

What do you like to do here?

Why come here if you have access to computers elsewhere (home, school)?

MARKETING

How did you find out about the Wired for Youth program?

Do you talk to your friends or other people about Wired for Youth? What do you tell them?

BENEFITS OF WIRED FOR YOUTH

Can you think of ways that Wired for Youth has helped you? (What have you accomplished?)

What do you know that you didn't know before you came to the program?

Have you done anything different because of the program?

If you were finished with the program, what would you remember most about it?

(*Alternate question:* If a dinosaur smashed the building tomorrow, what would you remember most about the program?)

Is there anything you wish you could do here, but can't currently?

Thank you!

Interviews

INTERVIEWS DEFINED

Interviews are question-and-answer sessions with an individual participant, conducted either by telephone, through face-to-face interactions, or online. Generally, interviews provide a valuable opportunity to probe and explore responses, resulting in the collection of data regarding library services that is rich in content and clear in meaning. Also, in the right circumstances (where trust and anonymity are established), interviews are useful to collect more sensitive information that respondents may not wish to write down.

INTERVIEW HOW TO'S

To gather data most effectively in a library setting using interviews, consider the following points.

Prepare an interview guide. An interview guide is an outline of the questions to ask, along with any probing questions (i.e., rephrased, reminder questions) that might help to elicit responses. The guide will help provide consistency in the administration of the interview. While it's natural to expand or revise your questions as you proceed with subsequent interviews, we suggest that you pretest your guide with a few users to "nail down" or confirm your questions so you do not have to vary them much in future. This will make data analysis *much* easier, and is a step we fully recommend with every approach—pretest your instruments.

Remember to ask permission from the interviewee, as well as further consent to audiotape the interview. Inform the participant that he or she is being audio-recorded and proceed with the interview once permission has been granted. Note that different organizations might also require specific procedures for seeking informed consent.

Emphasize the confidentiality of the interview. Explain the purpose of the interview, how participants were selected, how responses will be used, and whether participants will have the opportunity to see the results of the study. Remember and abide by the kinds of sensitivities that you identified for the interviewee in "Step One: Getting Started." Allow interviewees to ask questions about the interview.

Use active listening skills and maintain eye contact with the participant as much as possible. If you are not audio-recording, then write down responses inconspicuously and try to use the participant's exact words. Ask the participant to clarify vague or ambiguous answers; probe for specifics when necessary.

Do not be afraid of "white space." Participants need to time to digest your funny questions and form a response. Moreover, some people naturally speak more slowly than others. Resist the urge to rush in and fill empty space, and do not interrupt your participants when speaking or try to finish their answers.

Keep your interview guide to one page so you do not distract your participant by rustling pages.

INTERVIEW STRENGTHS

- Good approach to gather in-depth attitudes and beliefs from individuals
- Personal contact with participants might elicit richer and more detailed responses
- Provides an excellent opportunity to probe and explore questions
- Participants do not need to be able to read and write to respond

INTERVIEW WEAKNESSES

- Requires staff time and quiet area to conduct interviews
- Usually requires special equipment to record and transcribe interviews

In evaluating the New Americans and the Adult Learner programs for immigrants run by the Queens Borough Public Library (QBPL), we conducted interviews with fifteen administrators as well as program coordinators and volunteers. Interviews focused upon the development and implementation of the library's services for immigrants, as well as the generation of specific outcomes for their users. The following is an example of an interview guide that we used to interview program administrators.

New Americans/ESOL Program Administrator Self-Assessment

Scope Note: This protocol will be used for an interview with administrators of the Queens Borough Public Library System. The aim of this interview is to gain a better understanding of the role of QBPL's Immigrant Services program, including the New Americans Program. We are also interested in learning how QBPL evaluates its programs and services, and what type of evaluation would benefit the library most.

INTRODUCTIONS AND PURPOSE OF THE INTERVIEW

ROLE/MISSION/ACTIVITIES

Describe your own role vis-à-vis immigrant services.

What do the library staff want immigrant services to be known for?

What are the major challenges faced by Queens staff in developing and carrying out these services?

How do immigrants find out about the services?

How do participants use the services? (Specific examples)

What are the major challenges facing the participants who use these services?

GENERAL EVALUATION

What differences do these services make to the people who use them? To others?

Are your evaluation approaches to immigrant services different from the ways you evaluate other programs? If so, how?

What would you like to know that you don't know now?

What kind of evaluation tools do you need that you don't have now?

Overall, how effective are your current evaluation approaches? Why?

OUTCOMES (STAFF AND ADMINISTRATORS OF NEW AMERICANS AND ESOL PROGRAMS)

Can you recall a time when you learned how the New Americans Program had an impact on an individual or a group of its participants? How? (Nature of impact or outcome)

Describe (focus here on developing a series of examples of impact or outcome).

How did you learn of this? (Specific examples)

In general, how do you find out that the New Americans Program makes a difference to its participants?

What would you say are the other outcomes of these services from the perspective of their users?

What differences do the New Americans Program services make in the community? (Specific examples)

What are the impacts on the library of the New Americans Program services? (Specific examples)

RELATIONSHIPS WITH OTHER GROUPS

What kinds of relationships, if any, have developed between the New Americans Program and other organizations serving the immigrant community?

Can you provide an example? Please describe it.

What are the outcomes of this relationship?

Are there others?

What kinds of relationships, if any, have developed between immigrant services and other library programs?

Please provide an example.

What are the outcomes of this relationship?

In addition to the library staff, we also needed direct input from the QBPL program users themselves. Due to several factors, including language, we were unable to directly conduct these interviews ourselves. Instead, we relied upon program staff to interview thirty New Americans and Adult Learner customers—often in the language of the user—using an instrument designed by us to determine the usefulness of the QBPL programs. Translated into multiple languages (e.g., Korean, Chinese, Spanish), it purposely included short questions to minimize intimidating respondents (while maximizing recruitment). Individual participants were selected by the QBPL staff. The instructions that we gave QBPL staff and the actual interview instrument that they then used are given below.

Instructions for "How Libraries and Librarians Help" Customer Interviews

Who should be interviewed? We seek to interview people who use specific services of the library. At Queens, these services are those that are focused on immigrants.

Therefore, we seek to interview adults who attend programs designed for immigrant customers of the Adult Learner Program and others who participate in the New Americans Program.

You may wish to select a person you have just been working with, someone who has come to a program, someone who is waiting to use one of the ESOL computer programs, or a person you have talked with in the past. Whom to interview is your choice. We recommend that you focus primarily on regular users of these programs, but that you also interview some people who are less familiar with the programs.

Who should conduct the interview? This instrument is designed to be administered by staff who work directly with Queens customers.

Language. Since the majority of the users of these services are not native speakers, we assume that these interviews may be conducted in a language other than English. Please indicate the language in which the interview occurs on the interview instrument.

General instructions for the interviewer. Prepare for the interview ahead of time. Become familiar with the questions before you use them. There are only six questions, but we spaced them over two pages to leave enough room for you to write down the interviewee's responses. The interview instrument should be carefully stapled so that both pages are kept together.

Where to hold the interview. If possible, designate an area where you and the interviewee can sit facing each other. It will be much easier for you to write down their responses to your questions if you are seated. Using a clipboard will make it easier to write down responses if you are standing.

What to do before starting the interview. Before starting the interview, you must ask the person's permission to conduct the interview. "We are taking part in a study of the differences libraries make in people's lives. We will not write down your name. Can we ask you some questions? We will not make a tape recording of the interview. This interview will take about ten minutes. We do not plan to include specific information that would identify you."

Conducting the interview. Make the interviewee feel at ease. Ask each question as written and allow time for people to think through their answers. Use the probes in brackets as necessary. Don't rush the interviewee. Maintain eye contact as appropriate. Encourage the interviewee to continue responding with body language (leaning forward) and encouraging phrases (Mmm, anything else?, etc.).

Recording responses to interview questions. While we normally record interviews, we are not recommending recording for these interviews. Therefore it is important to carefully write down what you are told. Capture as much as you can during the interview. Allow time after the interview to provide additional details.

If you are told a story, please capture it fully. Stories are valuable to our research. At the bottom of the interview indicate the date, time, and language of the interview, what the person was doing when you selected them (e.g., interviewer had just been working with the interviewee, interviewee was waiting to use the computer, interviewee had come to attend a program, etc.), and where the interview was conducted (X branch library, interviewers seated in corner). Please write clearly so that our team can transcribe these interviews.

Thank you for your help. We appreciate your assistance.

Queens Borough Public Library Customer Outcomes Interview Guide

Staff member, first explain to the customer: We wish to ask you a few questions, which will take about ten minutes. You do not have to answer any question that you don't want to, and we will not include information that would identify you (such as your name).

Staff member, please read each question to the customer and write his/her responses underneath (i.e., no tape recorder to be used).

Thank you for agreeing to be interviewed. We want to start by asking why people come to the library. We think people have many reasons for coming to the library. We need to know more, so that the library can provide better services.

QUESTIONS THAT FOCUS ON PARTICIPANTS' NEEDS

Why are you here today? [*Interviewer probe:* What are you doing here today?]

How were you helped with X? [*Interviewer insert the topic just here*]

[*Interviewer probe:* Did you learn something helpful from coming to the program or session or coming to the library?]

Can you tell me more about what would help you? [*Interviewer probe:* What else would help you with X?] [*Interviewer, please ask for additional details after the initial response*]

QUESTIONS ABOUT THE LIBRARY'S HELP

What other ways does the Queens Public Library and its staff help you? [*Interviewer probe:* How have you benefited from the library?]

What does the Queens Public Library mean to you?

How did you learn about the library? [*Interviewer probe:* Was there anything in particular (about the flyer, person, etc.) that influenced your decision to come to the library?]

DEMOGRAPHICS

[*Ask only if the answers aren't obvious; DO NOT push the customer if he or she appears uncomfortable.*]

Age: 17–25   26–34   35–44   45–54   55–64   65+

Gender: ☐ Male   ☐ Female

Occupation: _____

Ethnicity: How do you describe your ethnicity? _____

How long have you been coming to the library?
- ☐ first visit   ☐ 1–5 months   ☐ 6 months–1 year
- ☐ 1–2 years   ☐ 2–5 years   ☐ more than 5 years

Who in the household uses library?
- ☐ husband   ☐ wife   ☐ mother
- ☐ father   ☐ child(ren)   ☐ other _____

INTERVIEW CIRCUMSTANCES

Interviewer, please give us *your* name, QPL division, and a telephone number where we could reach you if we need more information:

Interviewer name and contact information:

Interview date, time:

Language of the interview:

What the person was doing when you selected him or her:

Where the interview was conducted:

Please provide additional details as appropriate below or on back. Thank you for your assistance with this research.

Supplemental Data Collection Methods

As mentioned previously, you can use supplemental data-collection methods, such as observation and follow-up interviews, to verify and enrich the information and outcomes that you discover through focus groups and interviews. This complementary method serves as a valuable tool in both initial and ongoing outcome studies.

Observation

OBSERVATION DEFINED

Observation entails observing and recording the behavior of participants in a given situation. Observations can be a great method for obtaining data regarding participant behavior in a particular library setting. In addition, observation affords an opportunity to explore professional contributions, such as language facility or openness, in action. Observation can be considered in two dimensions: (1) the degree of obtrusiveness (i.e., from totally unobtrusive to complete, active participation); and (2) whether overt (participants know they are being studied) or covert (you, the investigator observes in secret or under cover). The rule of thumb is that you do not have to ask people's permission to observe them in public places, i.e., libraries, therefore it is fine for you to conduct covert observation. Indeed, if you did ask permission or post signs, then people might behave in unnatural ways because they knew they were being studied! It comes down to one's expectation of privacy and, again, different institutions and agencies will have different rules to protect their clientele.

OBSERVATION HOW TO'S

To gather data using observation, consider the following points.

If you are conducting research in the library or in an environment with which you are very familiar, you may find that observation adds little to your understanding of what goes on in this environment. However, if, for example, you are asked to build a web page catering to the needs of the community's immigrant population, you might decide to ask the ESL volunteer coordinator if he or she wouldn't mind having you sit in on a class or two as a means of beginning research to determine recommendations for the look, feel, and content of this new web page.

We recommend that you prepare an observation guide with which to record your observations. Decide what behavior or types of data to focus on. For example: what types of questions are typically asked during the program? What resources are they using in class? How is the camaraderie among students? An observation guide will help to consistently record observations and to capture the data that has the most value.

Observing an environment can be especially beneficial if librarians have the opportunity to conduct follow-up interviews and focus groups with some of the people that they have observed. (See the "Interviews" and "Focus Groups" sections earlier in this chapter for more information on these data collection methods.)

It is important to remember that practically all conditions under which people observe other people will be altered to some degree simply by having the evaluator in the environment as an observer. Keep this in mind when analyzing data. Be sure to note any possible influences of the observer on participants' behavior in the findings report.

OBSERVATION STRENGTHS

- Excellent approach to discover behaviors during library programs
- Provides indicators of the impact of programs that might be more reliable than data gained by asking people
- Good technique when there are observable products and outcomes

OBSERVATION WEAKNESSES

- Requires staff time to observe and record observations
- Cannot ask questions of participants during observation
- Follow-up interviews to verify observations may be needed

The following observation checklist is from a study conducted by Karen E. Fisher (writing as "Karen E. Pettigrew") regarding how nurses make referrals to everyday services while providing foot treatment to the elderly at community clinics. This checklist is very focused because she was specifically interested in identifying particular activities that she investigated in-depth later via separate interviews with the nurses and the seniors.

Structured Observation Checklist

Nurse Code:
Senior Code:
Clinic Code:
Clinic Date:
Total # Referrals Made:
Time at Start of Treatment:
Time at End of Treatment:
Description of Treatment Activities:
Date/Place of Nurse Interview:
Date/Place of Senior Interview I:
Date/Place of Senior Interview II:

1ST REFERRAL (DO FOR EACH REFERRAL)

How referral was initiated:

Observed reason for referral:

Name of service/agency to which senior was referred:

Type of service/agency:

How referral was made:

Description of nurse's information-giving:

What did nurse ask senior (or senior agree) to do next:

Senior's observed reaction to referral:

Follow-up Interviews

FOLLOW-UP INTERVIEWS DEFINED

Follow-up interviews are valuable tools when studying the impact of community and library programming over a period of time. Generally, follow-up interviews allow evaluators the opportunity to probe, explore, and clarify the responses from initial focus groups, interviews, surveys, and observations. Follow-up interviews can provide verification and detail for data gathered initially via some other data collection approach, as well as probe participants' behavior since last meeting them (e.g., whether they used a service, subsequent needs and actions, etc). For example, we conducted follow-up interviews with online community network users approximately ten to fourteen days after they completed online interviews so we could probe about their use of the information that they obtained online. This was in addition to the more supplemental purpose of clarifying and expanding their online survey responses.

FOLLOW-UP INTERVIEW HOW TO'S

To gather data most effectively in a library setting using follow-up interviews, consider the following points.

Participant consent to be contacted at a specific later date is necessary. We recommend that you ask for a participant's name, contact information, and permission to be contacted during the initial focus group, interview, or survey.

The initial data collected needs to be managed effectively so that the interviewer, when conducting follow-up interviews, can provide reference to the participant's comments and responses made during the initial study.

If the initial data collection was face-to-face, follow-up interviews do not necessarily need to also be face-to-face. Assuming the person who conducted the initial data collection will also conduct the follow-up interview, a relationship has been created with the participant and communicating via the phone may be just as effective as face-to-face contact in this situation.

Interviewing is particularly beneficial in confirming and complementing any data collected through observation. While valuable data can be collected through observation, the observer often generates questions that cannot be asked during the non-intrusive observation period. Participants in an observation study typically are more at ease during an interview than in other circumstances, since they will be participating in the interview with the context already familiar to them; they were the ones being observed, and they logically assume that the interview will focus on what occurred during the observation.

If you are interested in post-observation or post-interview behavior, make sure that you allow adequate time for participants to carry out any ensuing activities, but don't wait so long that participants forget what you're interested in.

See the "Interviews" section earlier in this chapter for more details on this data collection method.

FOLLOW-UP INTERVIEW STRENGTHS

- Excellent approach for obtaining time-sequenced data about subsequent actions, needs, and thoughts
- Good method to follow up on users' feelings and experiences that were shared earlier using another approach
- Provides an excellent opportunity to probe and explore with questions
- Participants do not need to be able to read and write to respond
- Can be face-to-face or via phone or online

FOLLOW-UP INTERVIEW WEAKNESSES

- Staff time to administer follow-up interviews is required
- Contact information must be gathered in the initial data collection process
- Special equipment to record and transcribe interviews is usually required

In the remainder of this section we share two instruments to illustrate the value of conducting follow-up interviews. The first instrument, the Community Network User Survey, is an online survey; the second instrument is the follow-up telephone interview guide that we used to gather further data from a subset of the survey respondents.

Community Network User Survey

This survey was conducted with 197 users of three different community networks and was based on Brenda Dervin's sense-making approach. See figure 5-1.

Figure 5-1 Community Network User Survey

Dear Community Network User,

We are a research team from the University of Michigan and the University of Washington. We are studying how people use Community Networks and the Internet. If you are over age 18, we ask that you take 5–10 minutes to complete the following questions. Please note that you do not have to answer every question, and that your identity will be confidential. Your answers will help us gain a better understanding of how people use the Internet to obtain information. You will find more information about our project at the end of the survey.

What are you looking for right now?

What, if anything, would make it easier for you to find what you're looking for?

For all past Internet searches, how often did you find what you were looking for?

○ All the time
○ Most of the time
○ Some of the time
○ Only a few times
○ Never

(continued)

Figure 5-1   (*continued*)

From where are you accessing the Internet right now?

○ From home
○ From work
○ From a college/university
○ From a public library
○ From a community technology center
○ Other

Generally, why do you visit the Community Network?

What else would you like to see on the Community Network's website?

Where else do you go to find information about your community?

To what age group do you belong?

○ 18–25
○ 26–35
○ 36–45
○ 46–55
○ 56–65
○ 66+

Are you male or female?

O Male

O Female

Do you have additional comments you would like to make about this survey or the Community Network?

Thank you for answering these questions. If this survey appears in the future, there's no need to respond again.

We will be interviewing people about their Internet use over the coming weeks. The interviews will last about 20 minutes and will be scheduled at times that are convenient for you. Interviews will be conducted by telephone, and your identity will remain confidential.

If you are willing to talk with us by telephone as part of this research, please provide the following contact information. A member of our research team will contact you soon.

If you prefer not to be interviewed, *please proceed to the submit button below.*

Name	
E-mail	
Telephone: (area code and number)	
Best time to call	

Please note that the information you provided will be kept in a secure database at the University of Michigan. Your e-mail identity will remain confidential and all identifiers will be deleted upon completion of this survey in June 2000.

Thank you very much!

Submit

Follow-up Telephone Interview Guide for Online Survey Respondents

ID Code:

City Code:

Time:

Date:

Interviewer:

Interview Length:

Web Page/Help for (based on online survey response):

Date online survey was completed:

Matched service provider code:

INTERVIEWER'S NOTES

Before we start, I'd like to explain what we'll be doing during the interview, which will take no longer than thirty minutes, as well as answer any questions you might have. Basically, I'll ask you questions about your responses to our survey that was posted on the CascadeLink. With your permission I'd like to audio-record our interview, as it will help me better focus on our conversation [pause for response; if subjects says "no" then interview will not be recorded].

Please note that you don't have to answer every question. This interview will be kept strictly confidential and your identity will remain anonymous when we write up the results of the study. Upon completion of the study all records that contain personal identifiers will be shredded. Any questions before we begin?

WARM-UP QUESTIONS (3–5 MINUTES)

1. How long have you been using the Internet?
2. How long have you been using the CascadeLink?
3. From where do you usually access the Internet (e.g., home, work, college/university, public library, community technology center, other)?
4. What are the primary reasons you use the Internet? (Keep brief)

MAIN QUESTIONS (25 MINUTES)

When you responded to our survey, you indicated that you were looking for X [answer based on online survey response].

5. What is the reason you were looking for X?
6. What were you trying to find out? [*Probe:* What did you want to know?]
7. How did you think finding X will help you? [*Probe:* How did you plan to use X?]

8. What did you do after looking for X (i.e., contacted service provider whose web page they were searching, began another search, nothing, etc.)?
9. Was there anything on the X web page that made you want to contact/get X? Why?

IF RESPONDENT CONTACTED SERVICE PROVIDER, ASK:

10. Did you do anything else before contacting X? [*Probes:* Look further on the Internet, talk to someone (if so, whom and why), look elsewhere, etc.]
11. How did you contact X? [*Probes:* By e-mail, telephone, in-person, etc.]
12. How did you think contacting/getting X would help you? What did you expect to get?
13. What happened when you contacted X?
14. What do you think of it? [*Probes:* How is it going? Is it helping? How or how not?]
15. How important was it to you to get help from X? (5-point scale: 1 = not at all; 5 = extremely)
16a. Apart from the Internet, how else could you have found out about X?
16b. Is [whatever] a good way of finding these things out?
17a. How often have you used the CascadeLink to find out about situations similar to X in the past?
17b. How often did you find what you were looking for?
18a. How often have you used the Internet, in general, to find out about situations similar to X in the past?
18b. How often did you find what you were looking for?
19. Is there anything that would make it easier for you find these things on the Internet?

[*Go to Closing*]

IF RESPONDENT HAS NOT CONTACTED SERVICE PROVIDER, ASK:

20. What is the reason you have not contacted X?
21. Did/will you ask around about it? Who? Why?
22. How do you think contacting/getting X would help you? What would you expect to get?
23. How important is it to you to get help from X? (5-point scale: 1 = not at all; 5 = extremely)
24a. Apart from the Internet, how else could you have found out about X?
24b. Is [whatever] a good way of finding these things out?

25a. How often have you used the CascadeLink to find out about situations similar to X in the past?

25b. How often did you find what you were looking for?

26a. How often have you used the Internet, in general, to find out about situations similar to X in the past?

26b. How often did you find what you were looking for?

27. Is there anything that would make it easier for you find these things on the Internet?

Is there anything you would like to add about what we've been discussing?

CLOSING

Thank you very much for participating in our study. I appreciate your taking the time to talk with me. The results from our study will be posted on our project website over the coming months.

Creating Open-Ended Questions
Aimed at Determining Outcomes

Throughout this book, we emphasize that library users remain the primary articulators of library outcomes. The interviews, focus groups, and observational methods discussed here enable librarians to capture detailed feedback from users themselves. Of singular importance, however, across all methods is the way in which questions are asked. In contrast to closed questions, which typically solicit a "yes" or "no" reply, open-ended questions require respondents to provide significantly more detail on their impressions of the impacts of services. Open-ended questions thus well serve librarians undertaking initial studies of services whose outcomes have yet to be identified.

The examples below include balanced sets of open-ended and closed questions used in our studies. They are designed to explore essential ingredients of outcomes, including the user's context, use of the library services, and outcomes. We offer the following sample questions as a resource to librarians embarking on a study designed to determine outcomes.

Questions That Find Out More about the User's Context

Public library programs and services serve an enormous variety of clienteles, from young people and families to service providers and immigrant populations. Once they have determined which users to target in exercise 4-1, librarians, being mindful of user sensitivities identified in exercise 5-1 (later in this chapter), can begin to draft a suite of questions aimed at exploring the user's context.

EXAMPLE A: TEENS

The clients are teens who participate in an after-school community technology program. Find out more about their situation. Without specifically asking the why question (often considered rude or too probing), find out what motivates the teen to come to the program.

> *Context questions:*
>
> Did you know how to use computers before you came?
>
> How much had you worked with computers/Internet before you came?
>
> What did you use them for/to do?
>
> Do you have a computer at home that you can use?
>
> How do you use computers now?
>
> What do you expect to get out of (name of program)?

EXAMPLE B: AGENCIES

The clients are agencies that use the library's information and referral services or community network. Find out more about the clientele of each agency and how the agency serves the needs of its clientele.

> *Context questions:*
>
> Please describe your audience or clientele
>
> How do you reach your clientele?
>
> What makes it hard for clients to access your services or get information?

EXAMPLE C: IMMIGRANTS

Remain sensitive to the collection of demographic and contact information about immigrants. Librarians can find out what motivates immigrants to come to the library by asking short, direct questions, in the immigrant's preferred language, that do not reveal personal information. *Contact information should not be collected; demographic information may be collected, with caution.*

> *Context questions:*
>
> Why are you here today? [*Interviewer probe:* What are you doing here today?]
>
> How did you find out about the library?

Was there anything in particular (about the flyer, person, etc.) that influenced
    your decision to come to the library?

Demographics:

(Ask only if the answers aren't obvious; *do not* push the customer if he or she
    appears uncomfortable.)

How old are you?

Note gender of interviewee.

How do you describe your ethnicity?

How long have you been coming to the library?

Who in your household uses the library?

Questions That Focus on the Use of Library Services

Library services are used differently by different people, and people may also use
the service for more than one purpose. In collecting data about use, librarians can
craft a set of questions to identify not only the range of users involved with the service, but also the spectrum of reasons why they use the system, as seen in the questions below.

EXAMPLE A: TEEN USE OF COMMUNITY TECHNOLOGY PROGRAM

Find out how the teen uses the service or some aspect of the service.

Sample questions on use:

What have you been doing today at (name of service)?

How do you describe (name of program) to other kids and your family?

If you were finished with the program, what would you remember most
    about it?

EXAMPLE B: AGENCY USE OF COMMUNITY INFORMATION SERVICE

Find out how agencies use the various service components. Focus specifically on
their use of the service and its component activities.

Sample questions on use:

How do you use (name of service)?

We at (name of service) call the agencies we work with "content providers."
    Do you consider yourself a content provider? What does that term mean
    to you?

How does (name of service) work with you?

EXAMPLE C: USE OF A SPECIALIZED SERVICE

The questions below are taken from a telephone interview of agency staff that requested GIS-developed custom maps. The interviewee was identified by a library staff member.

Sample questions on use:

We understand that you requested a map of [describe the map].

Can you tell us about the *situation* when you asked (name of service) for this map? What were the circumstances? Can you walk us through this situation?

What kind of information did you need?

What kind of assistance did you get in developing the map?

How have you used the map?

Have you had other occasions to ask (name of service) to (type of activity such as customized map)? *Repeat* as necessary for additional examples.

EXAMPLE D: IMMIGRANT USE OF IMMIGRANT-SPECIFIC SERVICES

Immigrants use the library for a variety of purposes, including educational, social, cultural, and employment assistance. Find out how immigrants use or will use a library program, service, or resource.

Sample questions on use:

How did you use the library today?

Have you ever gone to a (class or workshop) at the library? What was it about?

What else have you done at the library?

Have you had any challenges in using the library? Can you talk about one of them?

Questions That Focus on the Outcomes of the Program for Participants and Others

Remember that the goal of the study is to identify and to document the consequences, both positive and negative, of the user's interaction with the service. The questions here should target the participant's response to one or more aspects of the program.

EXAMPLE A: TEENS

Sample questions that focus on outcomes:

Can you think of ways that (name of program) has helped you?

What have you accomplished?

What do you know that you didn't know before you came to the program?

Have you done anything differently because of your participation in (name of program)?

**EXAMPLE B: AGENCY INTERACTION
WITH COMMUNITY INFORMATION SERVICES**

Sample questions that focus on outcomes:

What are the most valuable aspects about (name of library program) for (name of organization)?

How does (name of library program) help your clientele?

Can you please provide a specific example such as a success story? Other examples?

Can you provide an example of how the (name of library program) has had an impact on the work that you do?

How does the (name of service) influence your work?

Regarding the use of a specific service such as a custom map:

How did it help? How did it not help?

What were the outcomes of this help (positive and negative)?

Do you feel that (name of service) has had any impact on the relationships your organizations has with other agencies?

Are there things that you would like (name of organization) to do differently? If so, what?

EXAMPLE C: IMMIGRANTS

Sample questions that focus on outcomes:

How were you helped with (X)? [*Interviewer probe:* Did you learn something helpful from coming to the program or coming to the library?]

Have you learned anything important to you at the library?

Have you been able to read something that was valuable to you because you came to the library? Can you tell me more?

What other ways does the library help you?

What does the library mean to you?

Have you ever told anyone about the library? What did you tell them?

EXERCISE 5-1
Strategizing Data Collection

At this point in the design process, you have considered the contextual factors relevant to the study, the resources required for the study, and the data collection methods and questions appropriate to the user group of the service. To help you integrate these elements into a cohesive data collection plan, we offer exercise 5-1, which will provide a global view of the initial outcome study that you are about to undertake.

Using figure 4-1 developed in "Step One: Getting Started" and this chapter's insights regarding data collection methods as a foundation, in a table like the one shown in figure 5-2 you can begin to strategize data collection methods, such as observation, focus groups, or individual interviews, that will help to document important outcomes for particular activities. The sample plan in the figure uses the immigrant services example that was discussed in chapter 4.

Figure 5-2   Data Collection Plan for the Queens Borough Public Library's New Americans and Adult Learner Programs

Activity	Target Study Groups (including staff and users)	Logistics (how, when, where)	Method Used to Collect Data	Questions to Ask
English language and literacy classes tailored to meet immigrant student needs at basic, beginning, and advanced levels	ESL immigrant students	Short, volunteer interviews at the end of class session; all confidential	In-person interviews, conducted by someone they trust in the language in which they feel most comfortable	How have you been helped by this class? Name one of the most valuable things, if any, that you've read since you came to the library? Can you tell me more?

(continued)

Figure 5-2 *(continued)*

Activity	Target Study Groups (including staff and users)	Logistics (how, when, where)	Method Used to Collect Data	Questions to Ask
				What does the library mean to you? What have you told others about the library?
	ESL program coordinators, teachers, and tutors	After/during monthly program meeting	Focus group	What do you think the mission of the program is? Do you know how the mission changed over time? How do participants benefit from this program? How do you know this? Probe for anecdotal evidence that confirms outcomes
	ESL teachers and tutors	In class		N/A

Data Collection: An Integral Service Element

Collecting outcomes data is substantially easier when integrated fully with the library service itself. For example, participants in youth community-technology programs can be interviewed (or participate in focus groups) over pizza after they have completed a session or the entire program. Students are then revved up and ready to talk about the program. Focus group and interview data provide rich qualitative data; if possible, librarians should capture them on tape (but only after getting the permission of participants). Immigrants who come to a program designed to meet their needs for information about everyday life skills in America (i.e., understanding your teenager, becoming a citizen) can also be interviewed after the program. Individuals enrolled in English as a Second Language programs and those enrolled in adult literacy programs should be interviewed as well. Be sure to capture the stories that they tell and use the patterns to show how your library services are helping them. (We'll discuss this more in the succeeding steps).

Calling individuals who have used specialized community information services by phone may tell you how the service (and the staff) helped. The rule of thumb for telephone interviews of this sort is to keep them short and to the point. Providing people with postcards designed to collect outcome data (and including brief demographic information on the participant) that can be returned to the library may be another way of collecting outcome data. In short, in order to obtain the most appropriate data on outcomes on an ongoing basis, be sure to integrate data collection with your program or service.

Chapter 6

Step Three

Analyzing Outcomes Data

Earlier we introduced the contextual factors—the library, its service model and activities, professional contributions, and the clientele—that (along with traditional outputs) give rise to outcomes and point to data collection methods with which to investigate each factor and the synergies between them. At this point, you have harvested a potent heap of data, from interview and focus group feedback to observations and secondary sources such as library and program documentation, all of which requires analysis. How best to proceed?

In this chapter we present a step-by-step process that you can use as a guide through the very detailed process of qualitative data analysis. This step in determining outcomes may take some time, but patient and thorough sifting of the data will yield a set of outcomes resulting from your library's unique service configuration, and with them, an informed picture of the benefits that the library brings to its community. As mentioned in chapter 2, a "one size fits all" approach does not work with outcomes; the good news is that the outcomes are there in the data, waiting to be found.

You may, in addition, have quantitative data such as relevant outputs of the service (programs and the numbers of people who attended them, etc.) to incorporate into your findings. Quantitative output data help to substantiate qualitative findings. If you already know what your library's outcomes are, then they can be represented quantitatively, i.e., the number or percentage of participants in a particular program achieved a particular outcome. The professional literature offers a wide range of resources to assist with quantitative data analysis, such as Babbie and Blaikie.[1]

Analyzing Qualitative Data

The overarching goal of data analysis is to identify and organize patterns in the data in order to produce a tailored *outcomes set* that reflects the local service. At the beginning stages of analysis of qualitative data there is often a sense of overload. At this stage, however, you can also begin to recognize patterns in the feedback from interviews, focus groups, and surveys of participants regarding the "benefits [and drawbacks] to people as a result of your programs and services: specifically, achievements or changes in skill, knowledge, attitude, behavior, condition, or life status" as defined by IMLS. Such recognition is a very positive development. As discussed in chapter 2, similar responses across users point to outcome patterns.

The following steps can be used both to analyze the qualitative data that have been collected into an outcomes set and to capture the results.

1. Become Very Familiar with the Data

This introductory step provides you with an early opportunity to reacquaint yourself with the full universe of data that you collected. Read through all of the data and seek to understand the opinions and perspectives of the participants and to look for insights regarding the factors of context. For example:

> *The library, service model, and activities*: Where is the library? What is its mission? What set of activities has the library developed to respond to the clientele?
>
> *Professional contributions*: What unique skills, talents, attitudes, etc., do staff bring to the mix?
>
> *The clientele*: Who are they? What do they need or want and why? How have they been affected (both positively and negatively)?

When reviewing focus group transcripts, be sure to analyze the data sequentially (i.e., "who says what when") in order to follow the chain of thought and the reactions among participants. As you proceed through the data analysis process, and begin to scan and flip through pages, the familiarity you gain in this initial step will prove invaluable.

2. Peruse the Data and Begin to Identify Patterns

Patterns show a range of outcomes that are specific to the program but not necessarily unique to it. As you read and reread the data, you will see major themes (i.e., main categories of outcome) emerge. These emerging patterns or themes suggest the main headings in a possible report. These emerging main headings can be used to organize related subthemes. Consider, for example, the theme and subthemes we found regarding the contribution of the Peninsula Library System's Community Information Program (CIP) to building the capacity of social service providers in San Mateo County, California (for the complete report, see chapter 11):

Main theme: Capacity building

Subthemes: Saves time
                Reduces duplication of effort
                Enhanced decision making
                Enhanced grant development

Main themes and subthemes need to be substantiated with evidence. Librarians can illustrate the patterns they have identified with quotations and other support drawn from the data, as demonstrated in the California example:

Main theme: Capacity building

Subtheme: Saves time

> I think [CIP] is a great program. You guys save us a lot of time . . . [CIP is] coming up with updated printed lists of phone numbers; if they didn't do it we wouldn't have it. We would have to sit there and start from scratch.

> They [CIP] will hold the mailing labels for us and produce lists of providers based on a certain subject area. It's really a great service. I mean if we had to develop that list ourselves it would take hours to print out and type up and we can just call them and they produce it for us.

Subtheme: Reduces duplication of effort

> [CIP is] one-stop shopping . . . you can go there and have multiple needs filled . . . [Regarding CIP services,] They will get me the demographic information for the City . . . so that I will have a profile, they will do a map for me, so we use them for administrative purposes a lot. . . and they make it all pretty for you. We do not have the capacity to do that.

> CIP helps assure that we don't reinvent the wheel. CIP knows the information about the community; we don't need to know it too. We can go to CIP.

Subtheme: Enhanced decision making

> We get questioned all the time on the reliability of our information related to disability. And the more we can make that believable and have a clearer picture of it, or at least be able to define the problems, I think the better justification we will have for pursuing particular programs and finally funding them.

> And we have done some significant program development based on a lot of the information that CIP helps us with. They put [our data] in those wonderful charts for us and we get them just automatically once a month.

Subtheme: Enhanced grant development

> We have done some significant program development based on a lot of the information that CIP helps us with. We now have a Client's Rights Advocacy Program that is county general funded, a Kids in Crisis program, all not funded from but anything but general funds because we were able to demonstrate those were needed services.

> We have done some significant program development based on a lot of the information that CIP developed . . . the maps clearly demonstrated to the county of San Mateo, the county welfare department Human Services Agency, and to our agency where we needed to work on developing child care homes and centers.

Interpretations, of course, can vary. We *strongly* recommend that you ask someone else, such as a coworker (or two), to do the favor of reading and identifying themes in the data to see if they correspond with yours. This process is referred to as "intercoder reliability testing" and is a key element in ensuring the "trustworthiness" of your analytic approach and findings (see Pettigrew for more detail).[2]

3. Analyze and Organize the Data

The preceding steps have enabled you to integrate the data that you collected from observation, interviews, focus groups, user feedback data, etc. Now you need a way to organize the patterns and quotes they have identified into a comprehensive outcomes set. To this end, librarians can use software packages such as N5 (formerly Nudist), Ethnograph, etc., or they can place each heading and quote on a 4" × 6" card and sort the cards by hand on a table.

The aim at this stage is not only to identify and substantiate the outcomes but also to arrange them in a logical manner. The analysis always involves shifting data from one category to another. Remember that the goal of the process is to structure the findings—the outcomes of the service—as well as to provide support (quotations from users, etc.) for the outcomes that have been identified. When librarians have completed the process they will have assembled a core *outcomes set* and the evidence to back the outcomes up.

4. Document the Findings

This is an exciting stage. The qualitative approach you used to analyze the data and determine the outcomes of the service has helped you identify outcomes from the perspectives of those who use them. Now what? What will these findings look like?

What they look like will vary with how you plan to use them, as discussed in the next chapter, "Step Four: Maximizing the Results of Your Outcomes Study," but in order to be most useful, we recommend considering variations on the reporting formats that we have used in our case studies. Ways to capture the data so that they can be manipulated for a broad array of applications (marketing, internal assessments, etc.) include the following ones.

OUTCOME TABLES

These are a shorthand way of keeping track of library services' outcomes. Our tables of outcome include the outcome itself as well as the activities and inputs that library staff have designed and used to help to generate the outcome. We cannot overemphasize that the activities in which the staff engage are key to the library's outcomes. The analysis may cause you to rethink the way you and other staff deliver some services. See figure 6-1 for a sample table of outcomes. (Note that owing to space limitations the quotations do not appear in the table format.)

Figure 6-1   Sample Outcomes Table for the Peninsula Library System's Community Information Program

Outcome: Capacity Building	Activities That Foster Capacity Building
County agencies and organizations save time	CIP disseminates information to the providers and the providers disseminate information to the community
Reduced duplication of effort	CIP produces mailing labels which agencies request for specialized audiences
Decision making is enhanced, supported	Provides one-stop shopping
Grant development activities are supported	Provides custom-developed statistics as well as monthly charts and graphs
	Produces maps that visualize community data

FULL REPORTS

Full reports provide a record of the complete study. Several of the reports given in part 3 of this book include (1) the rationale for and need for outcome measurement; (2) the methods used to collect the data and determine the outcomes; (3) the models used by the library to develop the service; and (4) the candidate outcomes, and the qualitative evidence for them in the form of quotes, stories, etc. Since selecting the outcomes of a particular service is the responsibility of the library staff (and not that of the researchers), we identify the outcomes in the case studies as "candidate" outcomes.

Your full report need not look like the ones included in this book, but because it is the chief record of the work you conducted, it should clearly present the following:

> the purpose and scope of the study, including definitions of any terms or concepts that librarians think might be misunderstood. (Note that simple concepts which you think are self-explanatory may not be understandable to other readers, even if they are library staff.)
>
> such important contextual information as the library and the service model, including the activities in which librarians engage
>
> the methodology used to design the study and to collect and analyze the data
>
> the outcomes set, arranged in a logical way and including substantiating data based on the study (as shown in the outcomes sections of the case study reports in part 3)

Carefully developed reports establish the credibility of the data and its interpretation, especially for such audiences as city managers and auditors. In the next chapter we discuss the uses of the complete report.

PARTIAL REPORTS

Partial reports such as those designed for particular audiences or those that focus on a single outcome or group of outcomes can also be developed.

5. Develop a Database of Outcomes and Activities

You will want to maintain a file or database of substantiated outcome data, both positive and negative, by adding new comments, testimonials, letters of thanks, etc., as you receive them. These data can be arranged by outcome category, and will allow staff to better manage the outcome collection and analysis process over time, especially as you begin to incorporate outcome data collection as a natural element of library programs.

6. Determine the Outcomes That Staff Will Continue to Monitor

In all likelihood you will not be surprised at what the staff find as they continue to monitor outcomes. The outcomes are, of course, based on the activities librarians have developed to carry out the library's services and on the resources (inputs) that they put into the service. You may now want to regularly monitor some of these outcomes to determine the percentage of users who are affected by each outcome, as well as program improvements made as a result of your discovery of negative outcomes. Alternatively, the staff may find that there are certain outcomes that they expected that are not present.

In the next chapter, "Step Four: Maximizing the Results of Your Outcomes Study," we describe the final HLLH outcomes study step and provide suggestions for both the internal and external use of outcome findings.

NOTES

1. E. Babbie, *The Practice of Social Research* (Belmont, Calif.: Wadsworth Thomson Learning, 2004); N. Blaikie, *Analyzing Quantitative Data: From Description to Explanation* (Thousand Oaks, Calif.: Sage, 2003).
2. K. E. Pettigrew, "Lay Information Provision in Community Settings: How Community Health Nurses Disseminate Human Services Information to the Elderly," *Library Quarterly* 70, no. 1 (2000): 47–85.

Chapter 7

Step Four

Maximizing the Results of Your Outcomes Study

The product of "Step Three: Analyzing Data," the outcomes set, is a treasure trove of data that captures the library's or program's contributions to participants and the life of the community. Throughout the process, you examined the contextual factors that give rise to outcomes—the library, the service model and activities, staff contributions, the clientele and other stakeholders—to achieve not only evidence of impact, but also, and just as important, valuable intelligence from customers and staff about the nature and results of the library's services.

In this chapter, step 4 encourages you to digest this intelligence and to apply lessons learned as strategically as possible. After all, outcome-based evaluation stands as a key investment opportunity for the institution from which to reap the range of benefits discussed in chapter 2, including improved marketing, accountability, enhanced services or programs, and resource (re)allocation.

Step 4 thus helps you leverage your findings for external and internal review. In outcomes you find core messages about the library—what it does right and where it can make improvements—that can verify and inform librarians' predictions and intuitions and do the same for the community they serve. The outcomes set derived through outcome-based evaluation encapsulates knowledge of the positive and negative impacts the library makes on community life, which may differ or corroborate the kinds of impacts expected by library management and staff. Outcomes well equip you to step outside the library with marketing programs or campaigns for a wide range of stakeholders. At the same time, you can take outcome intelligence back to the planning table to ponder such questions as "What does this say about the service? Did our strategies and activities achieve our goals or not? Did we produce benefits we did not intend to? How did we do it? How can we do it better?"

In this chapter, we guide you through the following applications to help maximize the use of your findings:

Marketing
Accountability and long-term assessment
Improved services and programs
Resource (re)allocation

Marketing

In recent years, librarians have come to appreciate the value of marketing. The professional literature offers a range of insights and guidance on the marketing of library products and services. According to Janet Ross, writing in *Library Mosaics*,

> The keys to effective marketing are consistency, quality and quantity. Your efforts need to be both creative and professional. Your marketing objective is to keep your library in the public mind and eye, to be constantly visible in the most positive way.[1]

But how are we to articulate the library's positive value in a way that resonates with the public?

Targeted library marketing considers the perspective of the user. Whereas output measurements such as users served or revenues generated capture the scale of a library's contribution—an array of statistical operational data that the public may or may not comprehend—outcomes, on the other hand, allow stakeholders, including library staff and board members, funders, and citizens, to understand, in users' own words, "the powerful role of . . . libraries in our democratic society."[2] With outcome evaluation, the library marketer no longer needs to craft messages based solely on evidence of what the library does (its outputs). Rather, via websites, annual reports, press releases, grant proposals, brochures, advertisements, and at library board meetings and conferences, the marketer can broadcast to the world the unique value proposition that his or her library brings to the community—and in so doing, enhance the library's *community brand.*

The library's community brand is a combination of the personality of the library or program, what it stands for, and what it represents to patrons. Often marketers think about brand as an equilateral triangle whose three sides represent a product or program's attributes, benefits, and character. The program's aggregate outcomes can help inform us of its benefits from the perspective of the user and can help you to know which attributes are key to talk about.

Audiences

Library marketing, like outcomes, begins with the community. Public library audiences can take many shapes and sizes, from private philanthropists to collaborative partners and program attendees to bond issue voters, but all share a common interest in the growth of the library service. According to Judith Seiss in her book *The Visible Librarian: Asserting Your Value with Marketing and Advocacy*: "marketing is vital to [a library's] success and continued existence" and is "a strategic— and ongoing—effort to secure the support and participation of the community through effective communication of the library's value."[3] Outcomes may supply the message, but successful library marketing also greatly depends on tailoring messages to target audiences.

Remember that outcomes will be of interest to diverse audiences, ranging from internal library stakeholders to external community organizations and local, state, and federal government offices. Internal audiences may include

- library staff who are involved in your service and its activities
- library staff who are not directly involved in your service but are involved in other, closely related library services
- library management, especially those making funding decisions
- citizen advisory boards
- funding agencies with an ongoing interest in the service
- library board members
- community agencies that collaborate with the library and its services

Funding agencies, university and civic groups, local, state, and federal government offices, local media, schools, and hospitals constitute potential external audiences that may be interested to learn about the outcomes of local library services. For example, participants in the teen technology program of the Flint (Mich.) Public Library addressed the board of the William K. Kellogg Foundation, while in Queens, New York, ethnic media outlets routinely cover news of the immigrant services of the Queens Borough Public Library system.

Remember as well that people still do not understand the full range of the library's contributions to society. The following exercises can help librarians to target outcomes effectively to a range of internal and external audiences.

EXERCISE 7-1
Identifying Your Audiences

This exercise will help you to brainstorm a comprehensive list of internal and external audiences to ensure that as many people as possible learn about the impacts that the library makes on the community:

Internal audiences

    A. List the library stakeholders identified early in the "Getting Started" (chapter 4) phase of the evaluation.

External audiences

    B. Revisit the data and brainstorm a list of audiences. Read through the data collected in your evaluation in search of potential external audiences such as partnering organizations and groups, potential users, government offices, etc. For example, in our evaluation of library services for immigrants, we gathered data about the library's involvement with government employment agencies, local schools, hospitals, businesses, the ethnic media, and more. Each of these organizations represents a potential audience to which to market the findings of the evaluation. *Expand on the above*

    C. For each audience identified above, brainstorm related offices, agencies, organizations, and constituencies that may be interested in the findings.

At this point in the process, librarians must consider what specific audiences need to know about their findings, and for what purpose. Some outcomes are, after all, more relevant to some audiences than to others. The outcomes of the Community Information Program of the Peninsula Library System in San Mateo County, California, for example, can appeal to both social services practitioners who need and use up-to-date CIP information to match clients with services and to human services agency management whose priorities may encompass increased coordination, collaboration, and capacity building.

EXERCISE 7-2
Match Audiences and Outcomes

This exercise is designed to assist you in targeting outcome messages to appropriate audiences.

A. *Match internal audiences and outcomes.* In the first column of figure 7-1, list the internal library stakeholders identified in exercise 7-1. In the second column, using the outcomes set, list all the outcomes that each internal audience needs to know (and for what purpose). Outcomes will overlap across audiences. This step allows librarians to bundle outcome messages together by audience, which will be helpful in the development of dissemination strategies.

B. *Match external audiences and outcomes.* In the first column of figure 7-2, list the external audiences identified during exercise 7-1. In the second column, using your outcomes set, list all the outcomes that each external audience needs to know (and for what purpose). Outcomes will overlap across audiences.

Having matched audiences and outcomes, you can now brainstorm ways to inform target audiences of the outcomes they need to know and when. Possible marketing vehicles may include

newsletters

press releases

website story

published reports

flyers and brochures

news articles

radio spots

presentations to community
groups and the library board

discussion list notices

The resources that you have at your disposal undoubtedly will influence what strategies can be employed, but a broad approach can help to ensure that you communicate your findings widely.

Figure 7-1 Matching Internal Audiences and Outcomes

Target Audience: *Internal*	What They Need to Know
Library board	Immigrants improved their English language/literacy skills, and their candidacy for employment

Figure 7-2 Matching External Audiences and Outcomes

Target Audience: *External*	What They Need to Know
Ethnic media outlets, potential employers	Immigrants improved their English language/literacy skills, and their candidacy for employment

EXERCISE 7-3
Determine Dissemination Strategies

This exercise will help you create a marketing plan for your outcomes. Building on exercise 7-2, use figure 7-3 to determine dates of promotion and what kinds of marketing vehicles to use to broadcast outcome messages to target audiences.

Figure 7-3 Determining Dissemination Strategies

Date	Target Audience	Message (Outcome)	Marketing Vehicle
January	Local teens and their families, funders	Teens enhance technology skills	Library newsletter, website story
February	Local media, local teens and their families	Teens enhance technology skills	Radio spot

EXERCISE 7-4
Develop a Graphic Representation of Your Outcomes

They say a picture is worth a thousand words, and one way to think about getting your message out is to consider a graphic representation of your outcomes. Using a graphic allows you to sum up your program's impact in a way that is comprehensive and visually powerful. In order to develop a graphic, you need to think about what your outcomes say—what story do they tell?

Some things helpful to consider in creating a graphic include

How can outcomes be grouped together?

Are there patterns to your outcomes? Are they progressive over time? Do some seem to build on others?

How would you categorize your outcomes most generally—are they internal or external, short-term or long-term, expected or unexpected?

When you've figured out what your story is and what you want to express using your graphic, then you need to figure out *how* to tell it:

Is there an analogy you can use—some shape or figure that can represent your outcome patterns?

What graphics are appropriate to your audience? Is your choice within their frame of reference?

What tone, mood, and color choices are suitable to represent your program or institution? To appeal to your audience?

Figures 7-4 and 7-5, drawn from the Queens Borough Public Library's New Americans and Adult Learner programs and the Peninsula Library System's Community Information Program studies respectively, furnish useful examples of outcome graphics. Notice how each tells a story by illustrating the nature of the program impact and incorporating concepts such as internal versus external outcomes, outcome categories, and outcome progression.

Once you've developed a graphic representation, be sure to run it by a few people to make sure it's clear and says what you want it to say. Be sure to use a test audience that is similar in perspective to your intended audience, e.g., get your graphic in front of an internal staff before sending it to the library board or to organizational outsiders such as those on a community mailing list.

Figure 7-4   Outcomes Graphic for the Queens Borough Public Library's
New Americans and Adult Learner Programs

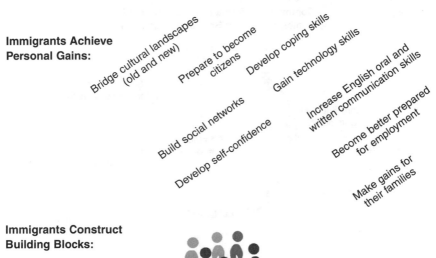

**Immigrants Achieve
Personal Gains:**

Bridge cultural landscapes
(old and new)

Prepare to become
citizens

Develop coping skills

Gain technology skills

Increase English oral and
written communication skills

Build social networks

Develop self-confidence

Become better prepared
for employment

Make gains for
their families

**Immigrants Construct
Building Blocks:**

Learn to trust library staff

Understand how library can help
Tell friends and family

Become aware of resources that can benefit them
Begin to gain information literacy skills

Discover the free public library and experience
a safe and accommodating environment

Figure 7-5   Outcomes Graphic for the Peninsula Library System's
Community Information Program

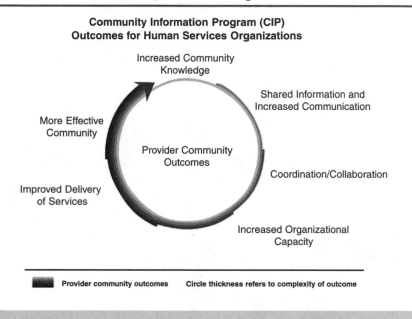

**Community Information Program (CIP)
Outcomes for Human Services Organizations**

Increased Community
Knowledge

Shared Information and
Increased Communication

More Effective
Community

Provider Community
Outcomes

Coordination/Collaboration

Improved Delivery
of Services

Increased Organizational
Capacity

Provider community outcomes   Circle thickness refers to complexity of outcome

Accountability and Long-Term Assessment

How do the library, its services, and librarians help the clientele? Has the library achieved the objectives it promised to grant or government funders? You can use your sets of outcomes to offer robust replies to these questions in grant applications, government and internal assessments, and more.

EXERCISE 7-5
Match Outcomes against Goals

This exercise can help to ensure that librarians continue to monitor service outcomes, and in turn measure accountability. Determine which outcomes to monitor for the long term and provide a date for their review using figure 7-6. Long-term assessment will help you to develop a deep and evolved understanding of the library's benefits to the community.

Figure 7-6 Matching Outcomes against Goals

Program/Service Goals	Outcome	Date for Review
Community Information Program	Capacity building for local nonprofit organizations	September + 6 months

Improvements to the Service or Program

How can the library and librarians be more effective in helping the clientele? Outcomes depict where and how the library is achieving success and, by implication, where it is not. For example, the teachers in the ESOL program of the Queens Borough Public Library system, a widely endorsed English language program, observed that the program's beginning, intermediate, and advanced curricula did not meet the basic learning needs of students with limited or no experience in the classroom setting. In response, the program designed an introductory basic literacy course to teach students how to hold a pen and how to write the alphabet, etc., as they progress through their English language instruction.

Librarians can make strategic improvements and enhancements to their services by examining their outcomes, both positive and negative, to determine

> What aspects of the program produce the kinds of outcomes sought?

> How might the library produce more of the most effective outcomes?

> Where did the program/service fall short of its goals? What aspects of the program need to be tweaked, changed, or eliminated?

> Which unexpected outcomes would the library seek to foster?

You can bring answers to these and other questions back to the planning table in order to enhance service or program delivery. (For librarians interested in using outcomes to plan new programs, see chapter 8, "Predicting Outcomes.")

Resource (Re)allocation

Should decision makers shift funds, staff, or other resources toward or away from the service? Librarians well understand the challenge of resource allocation. In an age of budget shortfalls, to invest in one service means to divest in another. Outcomes can help librarians make wise resource decisions because they indicate the benefits and consequences of particular investments. You can use the tables of outcomes in "Step Three: Analyzing Outcomes Data" to determine how best to (re)allocate resources, as seen in figure 7-7, an example from the Queens Borough Public Library.

Once you understand where new resources are needed, you can further consider:

> Where should new resources (staff, funds, volunteers, donations of food, etc.) come from?
>
> Do resources need to be moved from one aspect of the service to another?
>
> Is there a need for consolidation or other organizational change?
>
> Can collaborators be identified that can contribute or share resources?
>
> Is the service worth the resources that are being put into it?

Evaluation inputs, such as staff training and time, space, and materials, represent a noteworthy investment by and for the library. The product of the evaluation, the outcomes set, constitutes an initial return on the library's investment, one that can be widely leveraged to enhance the library's marketing, accountability measures, programs and services, and resource allocation, and one that can continue to maximize returns as libraries integrate outcome-based evaluation into their operations.

Figure 7-7   Resource (Re)allocation Plan for the Queens Borough Public Library's New Americans and Adult Learner Programs

Additional Resources?	Outcome: Immigrants Increase English-Language Oral and Written Communication Skills	Activities That Foster Increases in English-Language Communication Skills	Inputs That Foster Increases in English-Language Communication Skills	Related User Needs
Due to increased demands, need: More teachers/ tutors	Immigrants improve their English-language communication skills through	Fair and regular registration Classes tailored to meet student needs	Wide distribution of classes throughout the borough	To feel secure in the learning process

Additional Resources?	*Outcome:* Immigrants Increase English-Language Oral and Written Communication Skills	Activities That Foster Increases in English-Language Communication Skills	Inputs That Foster Increases in English-Language Communication Skills	Related User Needs
More space More materials	literacy and ESOL programs tailored to meet their needs	at basic, beginning, intermediate, and advanced levels Personalized attention at Adult Learning Centers Provide staff training, feedback, and support to foster increased patience with both clientele challenges and the process Multimedia, English-language collection development to support ESOL and literacy curricula Tutor training Low tutor/teacher-student ratio Conversation groups	Specialized staff Tutors Knowledge of TOEFL exam Technology Funding	Specialized staff Tutors Knowledge of TOEFL exam Technology Funding

NOTES

1. J. Ross, "Sending a Message: Marketing Your Library for Maximum Impact," *Library Mosaics* 6, no. 16 (1995).
2. Institute of Museum and Library Services, 2002 *National Awards for Museum and Library Service* (Washington, D.C.: Institute of Museum and Library Services, 2002), available at http://www.imls.gov/pubs/pdf/2002awards.pdf.
3. J. Seiss, *The Visible Librarian: Asserting Your Value with Marketing and Advocacy* (Chicago: American Library Association, 2003).

Chapter 8

Predicting Outcomes

Outcome Measures as a Planning Tool

RHEA JOYCE RUBIN

You have been reading about the contextual outcome evaluation model, which is an invaluable evaluation method with many benefits for libraries. Outcome measurement enables us to quantify all those warm and fuzzy customer anecdotes and individual success stories in order to document the changes in people's lives; identify effective programs and services; yield insights into why and how library services are used; provide empirical evidence that what the library is doing is what was intended; demonstrate the library's contribution to solving community problems; and energize staff by demonstrating the real, human impact that their work produces. It also provides statistics on the results of services for successful grant writing and fund-raising; demonstrates accountability as required by the Government Results and Performance Act of 1993; and keeps staff and stakeholders focused on goals and community context by stressing the *differences* that the services make.

For these reasons and others, funders of all types are now requiring outcomes measurement as a part of program evaluation. The catch is that applications for funding of *new* programs must include outcomes as part of the evaluation plan. The focus in this book has been on measuring the outcomes of *ongoing* programs, not on *predicting* the impact of new programs. You have read about interviewing participants about the effects of a library service, but what do you do when there are no participants yet? How do you know what impact your program may have? The mandate of outcomes measurement in order to receive funding puts us in new territory—predicting outcomes. Besides using outcomes measurement to verify the effectiveness of an existing program, we must also be able to state how a new program will make a difference in peoples' lives before we begin.

Because of this mandate, libraries are discovering how outcomes measurement can be used as a planning tool, as a bridge between needs assessment and the design of program activities. As chapter 3 explained, needs assessment is essential and must precede the determination of inputs and activities. Determining outcomes can force us to focus on the *needs* and *context* of our program idea; clarify the purpose of the program; compel us to make our assumptions explicit; and stimulate discussion of issues. It can also help keep implementation on track by identifying project milestones (or intermediate outcomes) and indicating when changes to the program are needed so that midcourse adjustments can be made.

Criteria for Selecting a Program
for Outcomes Measurement

Not all library programs or services are appropriate for outcomes measurement. An ongoing program is clearly outcome-based or not; again, if you are working with an existing program you can witness whether there are impacts to measure. For example, a retrospective conversion project has no discernible impact on individual users at the moment, yet a reading and discussion program for older adults may have an immediate and dramatic impact for some participants.

The new services or programs that a library is considering for implementation must have certain attributes to be suitable for outcomes measurement. The programs that are most appropriate are those that are user-focused; that aim to change the skills, knowledge, attitude, or behavior of a specific group of people; that contribute to a larger community goal; and that increase the library's effectiveness rather than its efficiency or quantity of products.

To see if a proposed program fits the outcomes measurement model, consider these questions:

> Has the program been developed in response to an *identified need?*
>
> Is *impact on the end user* a major goal of the project?
>
> Is the program more concerned with the *impact* than with the *volume of a product?*
>
> Is *impact on the end user* a major goal of the project?
>
> Is the program more concerned with *impact on the end user* than with *internal library operations?*

Is the program more concerned with *effectiveness* than with *efficiency?*
Is it focused more on *users' benefit* than on *users' satisfaction?*

Selecting Outcomes to Measure

Once you have determined that a program is well-suited for outcomes measurement, the outcomes need to be selected. In order to do this, you must first identify your intended participants. This sounds obvious, but most situations are not clear-cut. For example, a family literacy program may address a community need to "break the cycle of illiteracy." A library program goal—consistent with the library mission statement—may be to "provide coordinated adult literacy and early literacy services that encourage reading and library use in families that include low literate adults and their preschool children." The projected outcome might be that "children will enter school ready to learn to read." Alternatively, the family literacy program may really be aimed at the adult learners who are participants in the larger literacy program. In that case, the outcome would be that "adult learners who are parents or caregivers actively nurture early literacy development and the joy of reading in their children's lives."

Another example is a job information center created to address a community need to "increase the number of residents who are successfully employed." A library program goal—consistent with the library mission statement—may be to "help community members find or improve their employment." But the expected outcomes of the center depend on who you think will use it. What if the users are young adults who have not yet applied for jobs? What if the users are newly unemployed blue-collar workers looking for other jobs in their skill area? What about employed white-collar workers who want to change fields? As you can see, the intended users must determine the project outcomes and then the specific program services and activities.

Once you know who your intended participants are, the next step is to gather ideas on potential outcomes related to the identified needs. Thinking through an "if-then" chain of influences and benefits can help. Assuming that you do not yet have a program idea, use the chain from intended outcomes back to potential programs. For example, maybe your community has a goal of more employment among young adults, based on the issue of teens dropping out of school and then finding themselves idle. The library wants to contribute to the solution.

If we want more young adults to be employed, *then* they must be prepared with a high school education. *If* we want more young adults to graduate high school, *then* we need them to attend school more regularly and to get better grades.

If we want them to do better in school, *then* we need to offer assistance with their homework.

Note that the "if-then" exercise is a way of stating your expectations and examining your assumptions. It is important that you do a reality check by working on this with colleagues, not alone, and double-checking that the if-then phrases relate to each other in a reasonable sequence.

The if-then chain exercise can also be used if you have a program idea. Using the same example, if your library is considering offering homework assistance to middle school students, test that idea to see if it leads to your goal:

If students have assistance with their homework, *then* they will do better at their schoolwork. *If* they do better at school, *then* they will get better grades and attend school more regularly.

If they get better grades and attend school more regularly, *then* they are more likely to graduate. *If* they graduate, *then* they are more likely to become employed.

With a program idea in hand, check it out with others in the following ways.

Brainstorm candidate outcomes with the staff. Ask "Who benefits from this service or program and how?" Then, "In the best of circumstances, what other benefits might there be for those participants?" Note that talking to staff will not yield all the outcomes and is only a preliminary and easy step.

Interview or hold focus groups with current and past participants of a similar program. Ask "If this program really helps you, how will you be better off?" or "What do you expect to change for you as a result of this program?"

Ask staff at a similar program for anecdotes and testimonials they have heard. Ask "What do people say about the benefits of your program?" and "How do you know your program is a success?"

Talk with staff and volunteers who work directly with your intended participants in other programs at your library or elsewhere. Ask "What changes might we see in participants if our program is successful?" and "What do you see as the value of our program preceding yours?"

Talk with representatives of agencies that might be the "next step" for former participants. Ask "What will participants need to know or be able to do in order to succeed in your program?"

You should now have a reasonable program idea and probable outcomes. Of course, since this has all been prediction based on advice and logic, we are not sure that the outcomes we are aiming at are the right ones. It is essential to observe carefully once your program is under way and make changes to it, if necessary, based on the realities of the program.

Besides watching for any necessary revisions to your outcomes in the current year, look for unexpected outcomes and work them into your next year's plan. For example, a delivery program to people in their homes may be valued by users more because it alleviates loneliness than because it provides readers' advisory and reference services. In that case, the library might restructure the program to use less staff time; library staff members can provide reference and advisory services by telephone and trained volunteers can deliver the books and serve as friendly visitors.

Selecting Indicators to Measure

An indicator is a measurable behavior that demonstrates or implies achievement of the outcome. As with the selection of outcomes, the definition of indicators depends on the context. Who the participants are, as well as the position and mission of the library, affect the indicators. Using the family literacy example again, the indicator for the "children will enter school ready to learn to read" outcome might be a demonstration of children's emerging literacy skills such as the ability to turn the pages of a book or to recognize the letters of the alphabet. The indicators for the "nurture early literacy development and the joy of reading in their children's lives" outcome might be changed parental behavior such as sharing books with their children or playing word games and singing songs with their children.

Library Models

In response to IMLS' requirement of outcomes measurement, the California State Library has been selecting certain Library Services and Technology Act (LSTA) project proposals to include outcomes measurement. These projects have been given training in determining outcomes and indicators and then have written outcomes-based evaluation plans into their final funding applications. The following four examples can serve as models.

"Radio Works" was a literacy program for Spanish-speaking migrant farm workers in the geographically isolated area of western Marin County in California. From 1999 to 2001, the Marin County Library, in partnership with the local community radio station and other local agencies, worked with a bilingual and bicultural board of advisors to develop a series of bilingual radio novellas. These were broadcast as a continuing series and provided language skill training around basic life skills, such as calling 911, telling time, and job interviews. Participants received a bilingual "Listener's Guide" to use during the broadcasts to further enhance language skill development. Children's story times were also broadcast, and participants with children were provided with copies of the books read on the air. The project goals were to enhance English language skills and increase exposure and comfort with library and literacy services. Some of the project outcomes were positive life skills experiences (e.g., buying a car, attending parent-child school conferences, making a doctor's appointment) as a result of increased English language competency; increased parent-child sharing of books (e.g., reading together, attending story times); increased knowledge and use of the public library (e.g., getting a library card, attending programs, registering for literacy classes); and greater comfort participating in community activities (e.g., church meetings, back-to-school nights, community holiday events). The project was a great success. The library has just received a small LSTA grant to do a longitudinal outcomes measurement to assess if the impact of the program has been lasting.

In 2002 the San Diego County Public Law Library received an LSTA grant to address the need for access to justice by self-represented litigants in an efficient and effective court system. The law library is providing eight different classes on topics such as legal literacy, legal research, Internet and online database use, legal forms, and basic court procedures for self-represented litigants. Classes are held at the main law library and its four branches as well as at public libraries throughout the county. The project also offers legal literacy classes for public librarians at the law libraries and public libraries; enhanced legal reference and research services at all the law library locations, based on referrals of public library users by public librarians; and expanded outreach to governmental, community, and nonprofit organizations to promote both library services and referrals to the library. The project's intended outcome is that self-represented litigants will improve their legal literacy skills and improve their competence at accessing and using the legal system. Through a user survey and a nonuser survey distributed at the courts as well as participant assessments at the beginning and end of each class, an outside evaluator has found that the outcome of increased legal literacy is being accomplished. The project has received a second year of LSTA funding, and the library will continue outcomes measurement.

The Tuolumne County (Calif.) project is also in its second year of service and evaluation. A vast, poor, mountainous rural county, Tuolumne has received LSTA monies to initiate a mobile library and literacy lab in a vehicle purchased with private funds and local grants. The identified needs are building a sense of community for isolated residents, and providing services to families with young children and to Native Americans of the Tuolumne Band of Me-Wuks. The mobile library (called WOW for Worlds of Wonder) provides programs, materials, and satellite Internet access at weekly stops and seasonal events throughout the county. The services are designed to help residents overcome a sense of isolation by encouraging people of all ages to interact; and to stimulate reading to children, especially those in families with literacy challenges. The expected outcomes are that residents will experience a stronger sense of connection to the community and that parents and caregivers will encourage literacy by reading more with their children. A sense of community is an exciting and elusive outcome, but the preliminary evaluation of the WOW project shows success. As many as 98 percent of users surveyed "strongly agreed" or "agreed" with statements that "the mobile library gives me a greater chance to meet or interact with others," "gives me a greater sense of community satisfaction," and "gives me a greater sense of neighborliness." The evaluation will continue as the project enters its second year of LSTA funding.

The Los Angeles Public Library has just begun an ambitious program to better serve people with disabilities. LSTA funding last year supported a needs assessment, creation of an advisory committee, and planning by the library in conjunction with its community partners. Responding to the identified need for better resources and opportunities for people with disabilities, the new library program is comprised of five major components: the establishment of Information Centers for People with Disabilities at the main library and six branches; an outreach program to the homes of people with mobility impairments; a marketing campaign to promote library programs and services for the disabled; education and training for library staff; and an education and training program for residents of Long Beach—including employers—on the issues facing people with disabilities. The projected long-range outcomes are that people with disabilities will use the library to meet their information needs, thereby gaining knowledge and skills that provide them with independence and improve the quality of their lives; people with disabilities will have access to resources that can improve their employability so that they can be financially self-reliant; employers will employ more people with disabilities; and residents of Long Beach will be more informed about disabilities, thereby reducing hate crimes and discrimination against people with disabilities.

In all these examples, thorough needs assessment, involvement of potential participants, and collaboration with other agencies were significant aspects of predicting outcomes and designing relevant programs.

Part III

Putting Outcomes to Use

*How Libraries Contribute
to Individuals and the Community*

Ripples of Impact

Washtenaw Literacy Program Outcomes

MARIA SOUDEN AND SARAH WOODEN

Literacy is a critical aspect of the mission of public libraries. This cause can be supported through a variety of library offerings and activities—outreach programs, educational extension, classes, tutoring programs, and reading groups. Some libraries operate their own literacy programs, and some house and support non-profit organizations' literacy programs to fulfill their commitment. This case study looks at an outcome evaluation of one such program, Washtenaw Literacy, a basic literacy and ESL program housed within the Ypsilanti (Mich.) District Public Library. The outcome evaluation process and findings provide valuable insight for those wishing to evaluate basic literacy or similar programs in any context.

The outcomes experienced by learners in literacy programs extend beyond merely learning to read and write to affecting just about every aspect of learners' lives. Basic literacy programs touch not only their learners, but also reach into the lives of those around them—their families, their workplaces, and the larger community. Literacy program directors and staff are well aware of this—they hear the stories every day about lives changed, circumstances improved, passions discovered, and possibilities brought to light. These stories are often woven into literacy programs' communication with prospective tutors, donors, and the community at large.

At the same time that this very passionate, outcomes-based approach to fundraising and public relations has taken off and gained momentum, literacy programs have found themselves increasingly bogged down by the paperwork and required reporting endemic to some funding mechanisms. To justify themselves to funders, literacy programs may be forced to account for their success primarily in measurements of increased reading levels, improved test scores, and numbers of people served. The approach to outcome assessment presented in this book provides documentation for a literacy program whose goals are to actually improve the *lives* of learners, and not just their test scores. The Washtenaw case study shows that this type of outcome assessment provides a cohesive way to frame learners' stories in aggregate in order to demonstrate the program's overall impact.

The Role of Outcome Evaluation at Washtenaw Literacy

The context-centered model of outcome evaluation presented in this book was ideal for Washtenaw Literacy's current situation. Outcome evaluation looks at the impact of programs in the context of the environment of the organization, its staff, and its service model. It seeks to tell the story of program impact from the user's perspective. Washtenaw Literacy has been actively employing a mission-driven and relationship-based approach to fund-raising called "Raise More Money," which lends itself to incorporating learner outcomes. An informational video features learners' stories, the monthly newsletter and annual report both spotlight learners, and the learners themselves are invited to come and tell their stories at fund-raising events. The success of this approach has increased Washtenaw Literacy's community visibility and private donor base significantly. Based on the success of this program, the director wisely realized it was time to continue to refine the outcome stories they were telling into a coherent model.

Understanding Contextual Issues

In order to incorporate all of the contextual factors affecting outcomes at Washtenaw Literacy, we studied both the literacy environment and organizational aspects such as Washtenaw Literacy's service model, program activities, and human resources. We started with a scan of literature about literacy program evaluation, which was sparse, and reviewed several evaluation reports from other programs to provide issue-area context. Through these reports we got some ideas of what literacy outcomes might look like and what the issues around data collection were in literacy organizations and among low-literacy populations.

We assembled a picture of Washtenaw Literacy's service model and staff by reviewing its website, promotional video, and other communication materials;

conducting several intake interviews with the executive director; and attending a community informational session. Our team needed to be familiar with all of the program's aspects, but even for self-evaluation this type of formal gathering and compiling of contextual information is useful for contributing to the final analysis.

Service Model and Program Activities

The real strength, and the evaluation challenge, of Washtenaw Literacy's basic literacy program is its high degree of flexibility, tailoring, and customization. Learners enter the program at any time, with a wide range of existing skills and capabilities, and stay for varying lengths of time, depending on their specific goals and life situations. They are all starting at different places, and have different motivations for improving their literacy skills. After an initial intake and assessment, all of the tutoring sessions are one-on-one, arranged privately between the tutor and the learner, with content custom-tailored to the learner's goals and needs. Thus, the lesson plans for someone looking to be able to apply for a new and better job may differ greatly from the sessions for a learner who needs to know how to read and pay her bills, or get a driver's license, or who wants to read to his children.

As a result, Washtenaw Literacy doesn't have any prespecified, standardized outcomes for its Basic Literacy program—its aim is to help learners do what they want to do in their lives, not to achieve a certain level of reading comprehension. The staff and the tutors have a lot of appreciation for this approach to services and its impact on learners, and we felt that a context-centered evaluation conducted truly from the learner's perspective would help articulate patterns and aggregate these highly individual outcomes.

Staff

Washtenaw Literacy is sparsely staffed, with one part-time and four full-time staff members. Because of this it relies heavily on volunteers to support its administrative and program activities. Most of these are tutors, but typically an Americorps volunteer is placed in the Washtenaw Literacy office to work alongside the staff, and several of these have subsequently been hired. Understanding the volunteer culture of the organization and the scarcity of personnel resources helps illuminate the context of its activities. The staff members bring diverse experiences and considerable passion for literacy to the program. One staff member had actually been a learner previously, and most of the others have logged many hours as one-on-one tutors, and as such are very close to the mission.

Volunteer Tutors

Washtenaw Literacy provides a highly regarded and rigorous training program for tutors. They are extremely well trained for their role, with fifteen hours of hands-on literacy instruction that provides techniques and strategies for teaching basic literacy to adult learners. Training and support are provided on an ongoing basis through quarterly tutor in-services and monthly tutor shares. Washtenaw Literacy also maintains a tutor resource center at a local nonprofit center with literacy lesson materials and an experienced volunteer tutor staffing it. The tutors themselves bring a variety of experience and expertise to the process, coming with experience in business, education, and the professions. Some were learners themselves at one point and have additional experience to draw on in their lessons.

Clientele

Although learners who come into Washtenaw Literacy's Basic Literacy program must be at least sixteen years of age and at a functionally illiterate reading level, there are very few other unifying characteristics across its clientele. The Basic Literacy program participants are a diverse group of adult learners who come to Washtenaw Literacy with a broad spectrum of literacy skills, goals, and demographic characteristics. There is no typical basic literacy learner's profile. Conversations with staff and a review of literacy literature indicated that some commonalities among basic literacy learners include low self-esteem, difficulty in school or on the job, isolation, dependence on family, and a decreased ability to perform routine activities of daily living. The literacy level of the learner upon entering the program can affect perceptions of success and outcome achievement. Learners often enter the program after reaching a crisis point due to their level of literacy and are motivated to actively participate in the learning process.

Methods for Data Collection and Analysis

Once we fully understood the contextual factors affecting the Basic Literacy program, the team proceeded to develop a plan for primary data collection. We determined that our best sources of outcome data would be learners, since they had experienced the program's impacts firsthand and outcomes needed to be identified from their perspective. We conducted interviews with eight learners over the telephone to retain anonymity in the face of the sensitive nature of program participation and high needs for learner confidentiality. The learner sample was selected by Washtenaw Literacy staff to protect the confidentiality of participants, and consent for participation was secured ahead of our call. We requested that a broad sample of learners be selected based on objective factors such as tenure in the program, skill level, gender, and age. Additionally, we used the opportunity of a regularly scheduled Learner Advisory Board meeting to facilitate a mini-group of four learners who had taken on a leadership role. The sample questions used with learners are given in figure 9-1. These questions invoke a number of mechanisms to encourage learners to describe what they've learned, how it's helped, and how their lives are different as a result of tutoring.

In order to elaborate on learners' experiences, we also incorporated the reflections and experiences of Washtenaw Literacy staff and tutors. We talked with tutors and staff who had direct involvement with learners over time. We conducted three tutor telephone interviews and a focus group that included three tutors, three staff with tutoring experience, and two additional staff people. The questions used in the tutor interviews and the tutor/staff focus group can be found in figures 9-2 and 9-3, respectively. Essentially the questions capitalize on the first-hand experience of tutors and staff as they work with learners. Tutor outcome sets were particularly rich in that the tutors could report on the experiences of multiple

Figure 9-1   Sample Learner Interview Questions

What made you decide to come for tutoring?

What were your goals when you first came into the program? (What did you want to learn or do?)

How have your goals changed since you started the tutoring?

What caused that change?

What would you say you've learned in the program?

What have you accomplished so far?

In what ways has the program helped you?

What things can you do now that you couldn't before?

How has your tutor been helpful to you?

How is your life different since you started going for tutoring?

Is there anything that's happened for you as a result of the program that you didn't expect?

If you were recommending Washtenaw Literacy to a friend, what would you say about it?

What would you improve or change about the program?

Figure 9-2   Sample Tutor Interview Questions

What made you decide to become a tutor?

What types of things do you work on in tutoring with learners? What are the typical activities in your tutoring sessions?

Why do you think that learners come to the basic literacy program? What do they hope to get out of it?

What are their initial goals? How do those goals change over time?

How do you think the tutoring helps learners? (*Probe:* What do you notice that learners can do that they couldn't before?)

What changes do you notice in learners over time?

How do you see learners using what they've learned in their lives?

What are some of the success stories you've heard from learners?

Are there ways you see the tutoring affecting learners' families and communities?

What difference has tutoring made for you personally?

Are there times when the program doesn't work or isn't a fit for some learners?

Is there anything you think Washtenaw Literacy could do differently to serve learners better?

Figure 9-3   Sample Staff Focus Group Questions

What do you see as the core mission of Washtenaw Literacy?

What do you tell learners or prospective learners about the program?

How do you know the program is a success?

What do you see as the strongest aspects of the program?

Why do learners come for the basic literacy program? What do they hope to get out of it?

What types of things do they work on in tutoring? What are the typical activities in a tutoring session?

How do learners' goals change over time?

What are the most valuable aspects of the program for learners?

In what ways does Washtenaw Literacy help learners?

What does Washtenaw Literacy do for families? For the community?

How does the library benefit?

What are some of the program's success stories?

What outcomes or impacts can you think of that have surprised you?

Are there times when the program doesn't work or isn't a fit for some learners?

Is there anything you think Washtenaw Literacy could do differently to serve learners better?

learners. Their positions as partners of learners enabled them to take a step back, perhaps seeing outcomes more objectively and broadly than the learners themselves.

For further triangulation of the primary data, we reviewed twenty-five randomly selected learner files, which typically include goal sheets, intake assessments, lesson plans, progress reports, and various notes of accomplishments and achievements, all contributed by tutors and staff. From these we culled outcomes, activities, and driving forces. The nature of the progress report forms meant that they often provided "check-box" lists and short notes on progress, so we used congruent findings from interviews to elaborate on these items by interpreting and understanding detail.

We compiled the data and analyzed it for patterns and emerging outcome themes. These themes guided our in-depth analysis of the content of the telephone interviews and focus groups. Outcomes indicator statements were parsed out from the transcripts and entered into an Excel database, where they were coded by theme, category, and specific outcome. The data analysis is not quantitative or empirical, but every attempt was made where possible to triangulate outcome data—looking for recurrence of themes and congruence of observation between learner interviews, tutor perspectives, staff opinions, and learner file data.

Findings: Basic Literacy Program Outcomes

The outcomes experienced by Washtenaw Literacy's basic literacy learners are wide ranging, extending beyond improved literacy to affect other parts of their lives and, ultimately, to touch their communities. While the progression of outcomes is not the same for every learner, and one outcome doesn't always necessarily lead to another, there does seem to be a "build" effect, where initial or basic outcomes enabled additional, more far-reaching outcomes. We found it helpful to envision learner outcomes as a succession of ripples, as illustrated by the graphic in figure 9-4. The core impact is Direct [literacy] Results, which leads to the ability to make other kinds of Personal Changes, and then ultimately creates Extended Impacts that are felt beyond the learner.

Direct Results are the most immediate impacts of being taught literacy skills, and include two categories of outcomes—Improved Literacy Skills and New Literacy Attitudes. Personal Changes are life improvements enabled by increased literacy, and include Changed Self-Perception, an Enhanced Sense of Personal Efficacy, and Changes in Employment and Education. The Extended Impacts fall into the areas of Improved Relationships, Increased Involvement in the community and the workplace, and Literacy Advocacy in the form of learner recruitment, activism, and tutoring. Figure 9-5 illustrates how all of these categories fit into their respective levels to form a complete picture of literacy program outcomes.

Figure 9-4   Ripples of Impact: Successive Outcome Levels

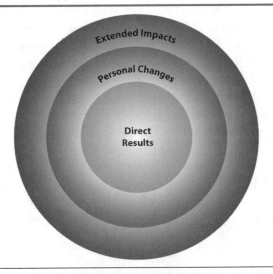

Figure 9-5   Basic Washtenaw Literacy Program Outcomes

The following sections discuss each outcome category in greater detail, including representative quotes from the data we collected, which served as our outcome indicators.

Improved Literacy Skills

Learners, tutors, and staff identified increases in the abilities to read and write and in associated literacy skills as perhaps the most direct outcomes of the tutoring provided by Washtenaw Literacy. These are core outcomes, central to other types of outcomes experienced. Learners could read better than they could before starting tutoring. They reported better understanding of what they were reading and had an easier time with words they didn't know. On progress reports, tutors noted that learners had progressed to reading books, newspapers, articles, directions, and correspondence.

> I can read better already and I've learned to read aloud. I never knew what a period was before, that you had to stop and pause there.

> I'm reading books that aren't easy-readers. I wanted to read some bigger books like adults read. I had to read children's books before.

> Reading the newspaper I can sink in more—I used to just go over it and not really understand it. Now I can understand it more and really read it.

Learners also gained writing skills, in both mechanics and composition. Those with learning disabilities and very low literacy levels had previously often avoided writing altogether, while those who could do some rudimentary writing had not imagined extending to more complex writing, such as letters, poems, or stories. With tutoring, learners became able to fill out job applications, write poetry or journal for pleasure, and keep up with correspondence. Other literacy improvements such as better pronunciation, speaking and reading aloud, and spelling and vocabulary gains were also noted.

> I've learned to write. It helps a lot. I write birthday cards.

> Her physical writing has improved and is much less elementary. Her name wouldn't even fit in a space provided for an application. (WL tutor)

> She is writing poetry now and I have helped her prepare some things for submission to contests. (WL tutor)

> I read my story and everyone liked it. Now I know I might be a good spokesperson.

> If I get to a word I don't know, now I can sound it out.

An additional outcome of working with a tutor, and perhaps a less anticipated one, was that tutors frequently identified learning disabilities, and helped learners develop strategies and locate tools to address them. Learners reported not knowing about disabilities such as dyslexia, or not knowing what to do about them prior to tutoring. They had typically had negative educational experiences where their disabilities were not uncovered or addressed, and they were quite emotional in interviews about the enormous relief that came from having a greater sense of realism and optimism about coping with their disabilities. The tutor relationship and individualized lesson approach were key contextual elements enabling this outcome.

> I learned about dyslexia from my tutor and realized I needed glasses to keep letters from floating.

> My tutor has also noticed a lot of things about my speech—I don't pronounce words right—so I have a lot of goals now, there are more things that I'm doing [in tutoring].

> It's let me know about my dyslexia so I can handle it different instead of shying away from it and making up stories to hang onto my job.

New Literacy Attitudes

Along with skill gains, learners frequently developed new attitudes and perspectives on reading and writing. As they gained competence, they began to place a greater value on basic literacy skills, and these activities started to play more of a role in their lives. Beyond just acquiring literacy skills, they were changing their attitudes toward literacy and its value. As learners read and wrote better they tended to become "readers" and "writers," spending more time on these activities, and reporting, to their surprise, that they were actually doing them for pleasure. On progress reports, tutors reported increases in the amount of time learners spent reading, and learners themselves noted that they were reading more and reading for pleasure, something that hadn't been possible when they struggled with the very act of comprehension.

> I pick up a book and read every day.

> I got really into reading books.

> I started a subscription to a magazine I have always wanted to read.

> It's more enjoyable to read now. Before I never liked to at all.

They see initial progress in phonics and the learners feel better about themselves and imagine themselves as readers. (WL tutor)

These attitudinal changes were also reflected in learners' new ideas about the general importance of reading. As they learned to read, and were exposed to a tutor who inherently values the activity, they started to value it as well. Learner attitudes changed toward libraries as well. Because the program was situated in the library, tutor-learner pairs often met there. Learners started to feel it was a place and a resource for them specifically as they got comfortable and tutors helped them get library cards and check out books. Staff and tutors noticed that as learners became comfortable in their tutoring, they might bring their families to the library as well, during their sessions or at other times.

I've learned respect for books. I never throw a book out; I pass them on.

I recognize the importance of reading. Before I wouldn't think of reading—I had to use other things to learn. I used to learn from movies and now I learn from books.

It is very heartening that learners become so familiar with the library. The library becomes a part of their life and they bring their children and families. (WL tutor)

I see them in here—they bring their families to the library. (WL staff)

Changed Self-Perception

There were a number of ways that learners' perceptions of themselves changed as a result of literacy tutoring. Some of the most moving moments of the interviews were when learners talked about shifts in how they felt about themselves that resulted from their participation in the program. Not only did learners experience increases in self-confidence and self-esteem, they had no trouble attributing those boosts directly to their tutoring experiences. These changes were described emotionally and emphatically by learners, and were influenced both by experiences of increased competency and learning success and an ongoing relationship with a caring, supportive tutor. Tutors were often cited as a direct support in changing learners' perceptions of themselves and their abilities. In addition to having more self-confidence and higher self-esteem, some learners reported an expanded worldview—being able to read and write opened up new doors and new possibilities for their lives. We were impressed at the avid range of subjects learners pursued as they gained reading skills—from geography to firefighting to complex accounting principles.

It gave me a lot more confidence in myself, that I can do things I didn't think I could do.

I learned that I knew more than I thought I did and could do more.

I feel more successful and more comfortable.

They feel less timid, have more confidence, and if someone is taking advantage of them they feel more assertive—they have confidence and skills to deal with it. (WL tutor)

I feel more sophisticated; I read more things.

I read everything. Now I'm learning hypnotism. Absorbing everything feels like a sponge.

I have the world, I can do just about anything now.

Success makes them feel successful. They don't just read in their lessons, but they'll notice they're reading paper more, or are more interested in world around them. Stuff at work makes more sense, and they find ways to use reading in all areas. (WL tutor)

They're trying new things, thinking about going places—they travel more—it's never been in their imagination before. (WL tutor)

Another self-perception change widely noted by learners was that by participating in the program they got some relief from the stigma associated with illiteracy. Being able to directly address the problem in the supportive, personal environment provided by the Washtenaw Literacy tutors went a long way toward decreasing the shame around learning disabilities or not being able to read and write. Learners frequently reported having "faked it" for most of their lives until coming to Washtenaw Literacy, and they found that the progress made in tutoring helped them access new energy, freed up by being more "out" about their problem.

Now I don't care if people know I have a reading problem. I'm not ashamed to let people know. I want people to know because I'm getting help for it and it's making a big difference.

I always kept my dyslexia hidden. Just to know that there's other people like me, that's a good thing. I feel more accepted; I'm not the only one with this problem.

I used to "cheat" at work, but now I don't hide it; I'm more open about it when I can't read something.

They're also frustrated about having to "pass"—the deception builds, it gets scary. They want to no longer deceive. (WL tutor)

Enhanced Sense of Personal Efficacy

In addition to new self-perceptions, learners also experienced an increased sense of their personal efficacy—their ability to make things happen. Learners were effusive about the increased effectiveness they experienced in various aspects of their lives resulting from their tutoring experience.

One of the most notable outcomes learners experienced in this area was a sense of confidence in their ability to learn or to further flex their new literacy muscles. This confidence was frequently manifested as an expanding of goals that quickly occurred as tutoring took root, and was observed by staff, tutors, and learners alike. Once learners had experienced some success with the literacy program, they had a sense of having many more learning possibilities and literacy activities open to them.

I am getting more confident—I would write to a senator now.

My self-esteem is better and I want to take a class now; before I never wanted to.

I've learned . . . that I'm not dumb, I just don't know how.

The world is opened up to them and they can do more than they had planned. (WL staff)

They get this tool and they start to find out what it can do. They just zoom into possibilities once they can read. (WL tutor)

Learners found that the skills they gained through increased literacy also allowed them to be more effective by becoming independent and developing life skills. They could do things on their own that they used to rely on someone else for, like go to the doctor or take a driver's license exam. Literacy enabled new life skills like shopping, paying bills, or banking that enhanced learners' personal effectiveness and quality of life. They also reported using newfound skills to impact their well-being, by accessing important health information and getting support for other personal improvements—they could read self-help books, or have the courage to seek out a support group. Some life skills were developed just through the process of participating in tutoring—Washtenaw Literacy staff noted that over time and with the experience of meeting regularly with their tutor, many learners developed a sense of responsibility around setting appointments and keeping them, being accountable, and being on time.

I can read signs while driving and I don't have to rely on my passengers.

I went to the license bureau and I could pass the test without having to have someone read it to me.

I don't have to ask my mom and dad for help with spelling.

Now I can read the bills. My husband did that before. He did everything for me. Now I have to do things myself. I feel more independent.

They can read medication labels and fill out film development forms. They feel so good that they can do things just like everyone else. (WL tutor)

I've learned to read road signs, even in unfamiliar places.

I can read a little better. I went to the doctor's office and checked the form they gave me for my address.

My learner is now reading aisle signs and not just shopping up and down the aisles. (WL tutor)

They can read their recovery books, and share in their twelve-step meetings more comfortably. (WL staff)

Continued Educational Endeavors

One outcome of tutoring for some learners was going on to pursue further schooling and other educational goals. We found education completion outcomes difficult to capture, because by the time they can go to college or get a GED (general equivalency diploma) often a learner is likely to have moved on from the program, but many learners talked about developing an interest in further education as a result of tutoring. Some learners started out with an education-related goal, but others were surprised by the desire to go back to school that emerged when they started experiencing success in the literacy program. Some of these learners had negative experiences with formal education related to their low literacy that they were able to overcome after spending some time in the Basic Literacy program. After improving their basic literacy skills and addressing their learning disabilities, some learners went on to complete formal degree programs such as GED, high school, vocational training, or college. Learners were also motivated to take additional courses of interest and reported confidence in their ability to pursue them.

I wanted to get my confidence back. I was told in school I could never accomplish anything. Now I have my medical assistant certificate.

One was going back to college courses he'd abandoned—in culinary arts. (WL tutor)

I feel better and more confident and want to take college computer classes.

Got a Career Focus in the mail and they have classes you can take, and I want to take classes in something I'd be interested in. I thought about taking a reading class at WCC until they find me another tutor.

Improved Employment Status or Outlook

Another outcome of improved literacy skills and working with a tutor is that learners gained the needed skills to apply for jobs, interview for jobs, get better at their jobs, and take on more responsibility at work. We found that employment crises often motivated learners to come to the Washtenaw Literacy program in the first place—learners were afraid to try for a better job or that they would lose their current job due to literacy inadequacies. Since tutoring lessons are typically oriented around real-life literacy applications, learning to complete a job application was an outcome frequently noted on progress reports, and learners reported great success in working on job-seeking skills in tutoring sessions. They also worked with their tutors on improving specific job tasks that require literacy, such as learning to read signage, understand instructions, or follow recipes.

I've been applying for jobs and before I would need help with applications, now I can do them all. Isn't that something?

Looking for a job—I'd been "babying it" for twenty-two years and got away with it, but I knew I couldn't with new job. I never thought I would be doing what I'm doing today.

It's helped with my job—I'm a driver and I can read the directions.

I made flashcards so he could learn the products in the frozen food aisle. It was one thing we could do right away to make him feel better about his job so he wouldn't quit. (WL tutor)

[A]nother was repairing farm equipment—these are complicated machines with computers, and now he can use manuals. If you're a farmer, you fix it yourself. (WL tutor)

Improved Relationships

The outcome categories in the outer ripple are places where we see other people directly benefiting from learners' participation in the Basic Literacy program. The increased literacy skills acquired in tutoring improved not only learners' own lives directly, but enabled them to have more frequent and higher-quality interactions with others, particularly family members. Literacy skills often became a vehicle for family connections as learners employed their newfound skills to read to their children or grandchildren and help them with homework. Another ripple effect is that as learners' skills and confidence improved, so did their family life—both learners and family members approached the relationship with a new sense of pride and learners were able to take on a greater share of household responsibilities as a result of tutoring.

> I can help my son now when he reads.

> I can read to my grandkids now. When I first told them I couldn't read they thought I was lying. Now I can read to them.

> He came in and told me how he'd helped his daughter with her homework. He was SO proud. (WL tutor)

> I had a learner who went to the doctor's office with his daughter who had always filled out the forms. This time he filled it out with daughter acting the "mother hen" and she was so proud. He was a success in her eyes and he couldn't wait to tell me about it. (WL tutor)

> People in my life are really proud of me because I'm getting help. My family would kick my butt if I quit.

> The family becomes really supportive. The families want to meet tutors and see the person helping their person. They have also probably tried to teach the learner in the past which rarely works out—it's too personal. (WL tutor)

> It helps in marriages—they feel more confident, don't have to hide anything. And confidence on the job puts less stress on the marriage. (WL tutor)

> When the learner starts working, it takes the load off the spouse. (WL staff)

Gaining basic literacy skills also gives learners the tools and the confidence they need to interact more comfortably in social situations. They were reading more, and felt increasingly confident, so they felt that they could participate. The sense of stigma that has often led them to believe they are dumb was reduced and they could participate more fully without fear. Tutors frequently incorporated correspondence in their lessons, and many learners reported better communication and relationships through writing notes, cards, letters, and e-mail.

Learners feel more secure with other people and new situations . . . they start conversations, track ball scores, and participate in intelligent arguments. (WL tutor)

They learn to speak up, get comfortable in conversation. (WL staff)

Then they come into sessions talking away about what happened this week. Just being able to be a part of the world helps a lot. (WL tutor)

My husband has a computer, and now I can use the e-mail. We met a really friendly couple from St Louis when we were on vacation, and he could show me how to e-mail them. I didn't know the words before, or what to click on.

I like to write birthday cards and now it doesn't take me two weeks . . . I wrote my sister and she told me I write almost better than she does.

I write letters to my family. I don't live close to my family. I have five brothers and two sisters. I'm disabled and don't drive. It is too expensive to call long distance. I can express my feelings this way.

I wanted help with letter writing because my brother has cancer and I was concerned about how I was going to communicate my concerns to him and how I feel.

The act of tutoring also evolved a relationship and a model for relating. Learners spoke highly of the interpersonal value of a steady and affirming one-on-one relationship with tutors. The customized, personal nature of the lessons and the highly application-oriented instruction meant that tutors became fairly immersed in learners' lives. Learners felt close, trusting, and supportive bonds with their tutors.

[My tutor] wasn't just helping me with my reading, she was my friend too.

Knowing I have support through them has changed me. It makes you feel good when you have people who care about you.

My tutor was really useful, and became a special person in my life—she was really great.

She made me feel better about myself too and helped me to read better and not give up. She's been a supporter too, a counselor-like.

Increased Involvement

As a result of their basic literacy tutoring, learners gained the skill sets and the self-confidence necessary to participate in the world. Their new skills and new perceptions of themselves enabled them to become considerably more involved in their workplaces, communities, or life in general. They were able to be increasingly more active and productive members of society. In the workplace we see learners taking on more active roles—no longer wishing to be invisible because of their illiteracy, and having the confidence to take on leadership activities.

> I needed confidence and it gave me so much I took on a team leader job at work.

> I had one learner who got active in union politics. Once he could read contracts, he started to investigate unfairness. (WL tutor)

Learners also got more involved civically and in their communities. They were able to stay informed, speak up, and have confidence to participate and take leadership roles. They became members of community organizations, and took part in elections. Sometimes this activism was based on involvement in Washtenaw Literacy activities. For learners who served on the Advisory Board, spoke at a community meeting, or helped get a newsletter out, these were often new activities and new roles. They experienced them first in the safe haven of Washtenaw Literacy, where they had built trust and been known in all their strengths and deficits.

> Getting involved in learner leadership is for some of them their first experience of being involved. (WL staff)

> I wrote my story for the [WL] newsletter. I never thought I could do that before.

> I attended statewide literacy conference in Lansing . . . I spoke there—it got me comfortable speaking in public, gave me confidence and an ability to coordinate and plan.

> I volunteered for two hours stuffing envelopes and I would like to do more.

> They are willing to volunteer and sometimes take an interest in local politics. (WL tutor)

> They are finding out about elections and voting. (WL tutor)

> They participate in voting and jury duty. I had one learner where I helped him read his instructions for jury duty and figure out what he needed to do. (WL tutor)

Literacy Advocacy

As learners experienced success in their tutoring, they carried the message of literacy into the world. They became role models, recruiters, and sometimes evangelists for literacy at home, at work, and in the community. As their shame evaporated and their confidence grew, they became natural advocates for literacy in all kinds of ways. They exposed their children to the importance and the joys of literacy by reading to younger kids and by modeling for older kids. Once learners were "out" about their illiteracy, it was easy to spot it in others and recruit them into the program.

> One day he comes in telling me he caught his kid, also a non-reader, sneaking the book down to read ahead. You don't just help one reader—you help generations of readers. (WL tutor)

> Kids get to see their parent reading, and that makes a difference, and they're teaching kids to read. Two of my learners had kids who were more interested in reading once dad was doing it. (WL tutor)

> They start being able to tell who are the non-readers around them—the ones that are using tricks. My learner told me he's trying to figure out a way to tell his coworkers about WL. (WL tutor)

> I wish other people knew about it because I know of these girls—at work and at my church—and I think it could make a difference in their lives; it has in mine. They can't read. I told one about it but I don't think she called, maybe some day she will. I hope she will.

> I've gotten people on my job into the program.

> I would say, "Please call them, they've really helped me." I would say anything I could think of to have them call—I'd give them the number, I'd give them directions. "Call them, you'll be surprised and you'll be glad you did. I'm living proof."

Some learners ended up being quite passionate about literacy and wrote or spoke as advocates for Washtenaw Literacy. They utilized their new skills to give back—writing their stories for Washtenaw Literacy public relations pieces, speaking as part of the speaker's bureau, and authoring donor thank-you letters. Some learners live that advocacy by going on to become tutors themselves.

> I talk to people for WL and I am 100 percent behind the organization.

> I am interested in getting into the learner program—the group [the Learner Advisory Board] that meets monthly to make WL better. I'm definitely interested.

> I am now a speaker for WL—I am a spokesperson and have talked in front of hundreds of people.

The ultimate goal change is wanting to be a tutor in the end. (WL tutor)

Tutoring another person has helped me as much as it's helped him.

My ultimate goal is to figure out a way to teach literacy where they can open a book and do it. I figure there has to be an easier way.

Tutor Outcomes

Tutors, in addition to being an excellent source of information about learner outcomes, reported experiencing a number of positive outcomes for themselves as well. This is important organizationally because it adds a piece to the context in which the basic literacy program operates. The tutors saw this as a two-way street, and derived intrinsic benefits from participation. Being able to help someone learn and to make a difference in his life was noted by tutors as very personally rewarding. Another, less expected outcome was that tutors reported being exposed to different perspectives or ways of life. Learners can come from very different socioeconomic and educational backgrounds, and being exposed to this incited feelings of appreciation or gratitude in tutors, for the material things they have as well as for their own perspectives on learning and books.

It makes me feel I'm doing something useful.

It's very rewarding to see them beginning to read.

I come home feeling good or excited about things going well. When you see a learner using things, it makes you feel good. You feel like you're making a difference.

Makes me appreciate good things that happened in my own life.

Tutors learn from learners; they get different perspective.

Conclusion

Overall, the Basic Literacy program at Washtenaw Literacy fostered numerous positive learner outcomes that can be directly attributed to aspects of Washtenaw Literacy's service model, including one-on-one tutoring and customized learning with content tailored to learners' needs and experience. Learners were surprised and pleased that they gained so much more than the skills they came for—they ended up with new outlooks and opportunities with which to approach their lives. They benefited directly from literacy tutoring, and as result, their families, workplaces, and communities benefit as well.

The texture and richness of learner outcomes that were reported provided the Washtenaw Literacy program with a great opportunity to harness outcomes for greater organizational effectiveness. Through the "ripples" diagram these outcomes are now positioned for framing into a cohesive and persuasive story for organizational stakeholders.

Chapter 10

Empowering Youth

Outcomes of Public Libraries'
Youth Technology Programs

In this chapter we examine outcomes that accrued to youth who attended after-school technology programs in three communities: Austin (Tex.), Flint (Mich.), and Haines (Alaska). The differing contexts of the programs examined in this How Libraries and Librarians Help study gave rise to a diverse range of outcomes. The Austin Public Library's program sought and reached large numbers of preteens, and the program was so successful that access to computers had to be limited to thirty minutes at a time. In contrast, the Flint Public Library's design limited participation to a small number of students who met twice a week for over four hours a week per participant. Flint produced an extensive array of profound outcomes in a small number of students (including teens who became highly skilled in using computer technologies and who made measurable contributions to their community), while in Haines, Alaska, youth mentors and adult mentees alike reported, among other outcomes, enhanced interpersonal relationships. As we have emphasized throughout this book, different program models and activities, not surprisingly, produce different impacts, but these case studies all capture measurable changes in the lives of youth and their community-manifested outcomes.

Contextual Factor One:
Public Library Youth Technology Models

The three case studies presented here, drawn from Texas, Michigan, and Alaska, concern community technology programs involving young people. The models vary radically, and thus contribute in different ways to the various outcomes experienced by the participants.

The mission of the Austin Public Library is "to provide open access to information and to promote literacy, love of reading, and lifelong learning opportunities for all members of the community." Funded by a partnership that includes the Austin Public Library, the Dell Foundation, the city of Austin, and the Austin Public Library Foundation, the Wired for Youth (WFY) program is an after-school drop-in program aimed at providing computers to youth in or near low-income areas in selected branches of the Austin Public Library. The goal of the program is to provide facilitated Internet and computer access to Austin youth, in particular those at risk. WFY is a nonstructured computer technology program for young teens and preteens based on computer self-use. The WFY computers, located in public spaces in branch libraries, are designated for youth use only. WFY staff "triage" children coming through the door after school, directing them to various activities and to computers which are loaded with kid-friendly educational software, Internet sites, and computer games. They are available on a first-come, first-serve basis. Most centers are staffed with WFY librarians who have the ability to teach multimedia, web design, and other computer skills. Each librarian acts as a facilitator, a reference librarian, and as an educator (primarily one-on-one, as needed for instruction). In addition, WFY librarians help students configure e-mail accounts and enroll in virtual pen pal programs with kids in other countries, showcase student work, engage in a variety of trust-building activities, and help students complete small tasks with attainable goals on the computer.

Flint, Michigan, is a rust-belt community that has experienced economic downturns in recent decades, including the exit of the city's major employer, General Motors. The city and school system struggle with scarce resources because of the declining tax base. The city is about 53 percent African American and 41 percent white. The Flint Public Library sponsored Community Information Agents Online (CIAO), an intensive after-school community technology program which required five to six hours per week for the school year and sought to foster teen civic engagement by giving the teen participants the skills they needed to help a community organization as it developed a web presence. CIAO participants needed to increase both their knowledge of the community and develop a range of technology skills. To this end, participants were required to spend one afternoon a week and a Saturday morning engaged in active learning and website development. Flint Public Library program staff worked closely with participants in the library's computer lab using project-learning approaches, fostering hands-on learning and team approaches to learning so that students could share their new technology-based skills with others and work toward the major goal of completing a community-focused website. They developed a mentoring relationship with the teen participants and fostered teen coaches to develop mentoring skills as well.

As a result of their participation, Flint teenagers developed new technical and communication skills, saw growth in their social and teamwork capabilities, and learned more about their community. By the end of the program, teenagers had adopted an array of computing technologies to support their project work. Hardware, including digital cameras and scanners, and software, including word processors, graphics editors, browsers, and web page editors, were among the tools the teenagers used each session. Students were expected to gain the skills needed to develop the content for a website by interviewing the staff of an organization and editing the website's content based on input from those staffers. The program focused on positive aspects of their community and encouraged students to learn more about their community and seek out community assets. Flint Public Library staff held periodic public celebrations designed to foster pride, self-confidence, and the presentation skills of the participants, as well as allowing them to exhibit their work. Students and staff invited parents, nonprofit organizations, local community leaders, and the local news media (including the local television station) to these events, which were accompanied by refreshments. Students had opportunities to present their work briefly to the entire group and demonstrate it at one of the computer stations in the lab.

In Alaska, the Dragonfly Project, an initiative of the Chilkoot Indian Association and the Haines Borough Public Library Technology Awareness Program (funded by IMLS), states its hope that "by helping young people teach adults the ways of computer technology, lives will be transformed." Named after the dragonfly, thought in local Tlingit mythology to be a transport of the human soul and a symbol of transformation, this program trains young people to share their technology skills with the Native American community and the general public. The project simultaneously engages two audiences: twenty tech-savvy young people aged eleven to twenty-one who train as mentors to teach the public how to use the library's technology and resources, to develop materials and techniques to teach concepts and skills on a one-to-one basis, and to conduct community outreach; and their students, hundreds of adults in the community who wish to improve their technology skills. The program supplies appropriate hardware and software tools and sponsors technology awareness nights at the library, as well as instruction by appointment. To date, Dragonfly mentors have developed curricula for a variety of software and technology programs, including Microsoft Excel, PowerPoint, Word, Publisher (with which to design resumes), as well as the library's public access catalog. Students can practice their skills at the library or at home on a range of projects, such as setting up spreadsheets for business or personal use, developing a database of family recipes, creating greetings cards, flyers, brochures, and business cards, and searching the Internet for job postings and the latest news on stocks.

Professional Contributions

Austin's Wired for Youth program is staffed by recent L.I.S. graduates who possess technology skills and an interest in youth and are supervised by a seasoned expert in youth services. The WFY model is based in library branches that serve at-risk youth and has been shaped by each WFY librarian. At the time of our visit the computers shared a set of software, but the approaches used were those developed by each librarian and were shared at monthly staff meetings. The staff created a warm, welcoming atmosphere, had a sense of humor, and were good communicators.

Flint's CIAO program tapped the skills of three otherwise very busy librarians—the head of children's services, the young adult librarian, and the cybrarian—all of whom had other major library responsibilities. External funding provided stipends for participants and two graduate students from the University of Michigan who provided additional technology and training skills and served part-time as coaches.

Flint Public Library staff made connections with relevant community organizations and used their own knowledge of the community to give students the connections they needed with community nonprofit organizations. Two mentors who had participated in a previous iteration of this program acted as student mentors. The staff shared the strong interpersonal qualities seen in Austin. They fostered participant learning about the community and civic engagement; they were generous with their time and community connections; they worked with kids to develop celebrations of accomplishments, including community-wide publicity (coverage on the local news); and they provided the opportunity for teens to assume responsibilities.

The staff of the Haines Public Library bring broad educational knowledge and experience to their mix. The library's education coordinator works with each mentor to develop his or her teaching and curriculum development skills. During their training, teen mentors serve as teaching assistants and conduct one-on-one mentoring sessions to probe the needs and wishes of the mentee. Mentors then bring these insights back to the table to revise the project's curricula in order to respond better to individual learning styles and to test revised curricular approaches. The staff additionally support the program's outreach efforts through links to local radio and newspaper outlets. The Haines staff help to create an informal and welcoming learning environment and to encourage participants to pursue their dreams, key attitudinal assets that contribute to the positive outcomes of the program.

Contextual Factor Two: Local Youth

The Austin Public Library's Wired for Youth Centers target youth between the ages of nine and thirteen. Recruitment is specific to each WFY Center. Some centers are located across from local schools, making them a natural choice for youth searching for a place to spend after-school hours. One WFY participant told the research team that until recently he had waited for his mother at a location between his school and the public library. A police officer told him that location was not a safe place and suggested other spots to wait, including the public library. The student went to the public library and discovered the WFY Center; now he goes to the center most days after school. A WFY staff member indicated, "In this one branch that now has eighty kids every day after school, these kids were previously hanging out on the streets after school." The response to this program has been so great in multiple branches that often large numbers of children seeking access to the computers exceed the capability of the branch to serve them, necessitating alternate strategies. As a result of the large response to the program, staff schedule computer use in thirty-minute blocks and devise means to otherwise engage children who wait their turn. This strategy increases the total number of users—and thus the number of children who gain benefits from the program—but the time limit set by the library influences the overall range of outcomes that can accrue to individual kids.

On the other hand, the Flint Public Library's CIAO program, which sought to teach a small group of high school students information access and computer technology as tools for change, rationed the number of students in the program. CIAO participants were suggested first by high school counselors who identified them as kids with potential for growth. They were then interviewed by CIAO staff and "hired" as community information agents by the public library. Each of the participants worked closely with staff, with other participants, and on their own for at least five hours per week, focusing on gaining computer facility and learning more about their community.

Consistent with its mission "to be responsive to community needs by assembling, preserving and administering materials and providing access to information via telecommunications where appropriate," the Dragonfly Project has served hundreds of residents of the Haines Borough of Alaska, a small northern community that is home to 2,400 people of whom, according to the 2000 census, 15 percent claim American Indian or Alaska Native ancestry. Approximately 23 percent of Haines Borough residents fall under the age of twenty-five, a key demographic factor for a project designed to "commingle" local youth and adults. Participants learn about the project via the Haines Public Library website and project publications developed by the staff, and through word-of-mouth and coverage in the local newspaper and on radio broadcasts.

Outcomes of Youth Technology Programs in Public Libraries

Our study of after-school community technology programs in Flint and Austin and the Dragonfly outcome assessment conducted by the Haines Public Library show that such public library programs can have strong impacts on the young people who use them. Not only do these programs increase computer and Internet skills (that's why the youth participate), but they produce a number of other outcomes as well. Given the differences in the programs' models and the fact that in determining program impacts a "one size fits all" approach does not apply, their outcomes are not the same. They may vary both in kind and intensity while the overall framework may be similar. Each of the *italicized phrases* in the following sections represents a major category of outcomes which are often accompanied by a range of indicators of impact.

Austin Outcomes

Wired for Youth Centers have become a safe place for kids after school, and many stay until the library closes. Youth interviewed at the library told us how much they valued it as a safe, welcoming place where they could do homework, work and play on the computers, and work with others. Not surprisingly, students increased their technology skills (see figure 10-1). Kids who use WFY value the program because it fosters their ability to learn. "I love the library because [name of staff member] helps me with my homework and I get to use the computers," one fifth-grader exclaimed. Participating in WFY has given Austin children the opportunity to increase their communication and self-expression skills. For example, one said "I sent a card to my friend from Peru. I know her from the computer . . .

Figure 10-1   Outcomes of the "Wired for Youth" Community Technology Program

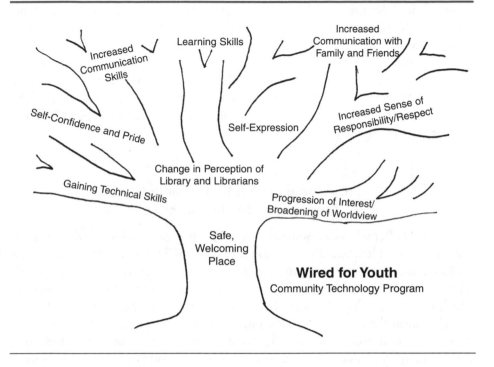

[Name of staff member] helped us set it up." Perception and attitude changes such as increasing trust of library staff are other important outcomes of this program. For kids who have negative perceptions of adults in their lives, changed perceptions are necessary before they can trust an adult. One youth's comments reflected such a change:

> This library would be no good without [name of staff member] . . . [Name of staff member] is the only reason I come. This library would suck because I don't like the people out there, because they're mean; they don't let you do nothing . . . [Name of staff member] can always help you.

Wired for Youth librarians noticed that over time the program *helped build the children's confidence and broaden children's worldview*. The research team attended a "girls' night out" program sponsored by a WFY Center. This program provided an opportunity for the kids to think about their future and hear other people's experiences.

> Last time six ladies came and they asked us what we wanted to be when we grow up. They told us their experiences, when they were younger. One was in the Army and she went to different places and worked in different places.

This research showed that *benefits extend beyond the participants* to their families and friends. WFY participants have brought their e-mail skills home and shared them with their families, who use the technology to communicate with family members in other locations.

> E-mail is important too, because we have an Aunty who lives in Los Angeles, and sometimes we can't talk on the phone . . . My Aunty says she get e-mails. She sends us postcards.

The candidate outcomes of the Wired for Youth program are shown in figure 10-2, along with the activities and inputs that generated them.

Figure 10-2 Candidate Outcomes of the
Austin Public Library's "Wired for Youth" Program*

Outcome: Gaining Technical Skills	Activities That Foster Technical Skill Development	Inputs That Foster Technical Skill Development**
Learned how to use a computer	Hands-on instruction	A computer lab with Internet access
Learned how to use selected software products	Encouraged participants to use technology to express themselves	Software including: website development tools, web browser, Swish, 16 colors, games
Evaluated the quality of Internet resources	Used humor to teach technology concepts	
Learned how to create a website	Participants are encouraged to work together	Color printer
Learned about various useful and interesting websites		Staff with technical skills
Knowledge of how to reboot the computer		Staff with children's instructional skills

* Outcomes in the first column are the result of activities and inputs in columns 2 and 3.
** Some of the inputs in column 3 are consistent and won't be repeated for the sake of brevity.

(*continued*)

Figure 10-2   *(continued)*

Outcome: Learning Skills	Activities That Foster Learning Skills	Inputs That Foster Learning Skills
Kids choose to help younger kids Information exchange, including exchange of URLs Enhanced knowledge/learning Kids work on or complete homework	Create a mentoring relationship with youth Provide a place for youth to work on homework with staff	Staff with children's instructional skills Library collections VICTORY program tutors
Outcome: Increased Communication Skills	**Activities That Foster Increased Communication Skills**	**Inputs That Foster Increased Communication Skills**
The ability to use the computer to communicate with others via e-mail Participants practice their writing skills Children, many of whom speak Spanish, become able to communicate with children in other countries	Librarians help kids configure e-mail accounts Helping participants enroll in virtual pen pal programs	Welcoming, friendly staff Computer lab with Internet access Time for staff and kids to interact
Outcome: Progression of Interest/ Broadening of Worldview	**Activities That Foster Progression of Interest/ Broadening of Worldview**	**Inputs That Foster Progression of Interest/ Broadening of Worldview**
Participants experience heightened awareness of self, community, other cultures Awareness of new career options Improved ability to relate to adults, community	Participants communicate with children in other countries, cultures Participants listen to women speak about different career options Librarian invites "girls' night out" speakers Helping participants enroll in virtual pen pal programs Participants are encouraged to communicate with other children	Staff with teaching ability, broad worldview Computer lab with Internet access Having a room that can accommodate a speaker E-mail access

Outcome: Self-Expression	Activities That Foster Self-Expression	Inputs That Foster Self-Expression
Increased sense of self Creative self-expression	Allowing children to use center materials to express their creativity Showcasing student creations in the center	Welcoming, friendly staff Software that fosters writing, art, creativity
Outcome: Change in Perception of Library and Librarians	**Activities That Foster Change in Perception of Library and Librarians**	**Inputs That Foster Change in Perception of Library and Librarians**
Increased comfort with being in the library Changed perception of librarians as trusted adults	Provided time for librarians and participants to interact Willingness to spend time with participant and family Expressing interest in participants' lives and activities Building trust Providing small snacks to kids	Welcoming, friendly staff Food Staff who do not match librarian stereotypes Time for staff and kids to interact
Outcome: Self-Confidence and Pride	**Activities That Foster Self-Confidence and Pride**	**Inputs That Foster Self-Confidence and Pride**
Self-confidence and pride A shift in peer attitudes and respect	Completing small tasks on the computer with attainable goals	Welcoming, friendly staff Computer lab, easy-to-use software Time for staff and kids to interact
Outcomes of Increased Sense of Responsibility/ Respect	**Activities for Increased Sense of Responsibility/ Respect**	**Inputs for Increased Sense of Responsibility/Respect**
Increased sense of responsibility/respect Participants want to make the librarians proud of them Youth feel useful to the WFY program	Librarians creatively utilize helpful youth Assigning youth simple tasks, such as signing up kids for computers, rebooting Celebrating participants' achievements	Welcoming, friendly staff Time for staff and kids to interact

(*continued*)

Figure 10-2   *(continued)*

Outcome: Safe Place	Activities That Foster Safe Place	Inputs That Foster Safe Place
A lasting impression that the library is a safe place for children Children spend time at the library rather than in less desirable places or more dangerous pursuits	Promoting library as a welcoming place for neighborhood children Informal environment A staff member is assigned to "triage" children coming through the door into various programs, areas	Clean, well-maintained inviting library building Visible computers Welcoming, friendly staff Branches located close to where children are: near schools, drop-in centers
Outcome: Increased Communication with Families and Friends	**Activities/Strategies for Increased Communication with Families and Friends**	**Inputs That Foster Increased Communication with Families and Friends**
Family, teachers, friends of WFY participants gain technology skills Technology is used to communicate with friends, family members in other locations	Participants share their knowledge with their families, teachers, and others in the community Staff talk to families of children who visit centers about resources and options	Welcoming, friendly staff Perception of library as safe place Computer lab with Internet access Time for staff to interact with families and kids

Flint Outcomes

The teens that participated in the Community Information Agents Online (CIAO) program in Flint gained a range of *technology skills.* (See figure 10-3.) Gaining these skills provided the teens with personal recognition. They likewise developed *communication skills,* including the ability to express themselves and to communicate more effectively with people they didn't know well. One participant noted:

> [Before CIAO when] speaking to people, I was more kind of an antisocial person. When I first started, I really didn't talk to people I don't know well. I'd have to completely just know you for so long before I'd talk to you. Now I can talk to almost anybody about anything no matter where I am.

Flint CIAO participants made a variety of learning gains. Participants became *actively engaged in their own learning and gained knowledge of their community.* One participant told us:

> I was interested in computers to begin with. So, learning how to work with web pages and work on the Internet and then working with the different community

Figure 10-3   Outcomes of the CIAO Program

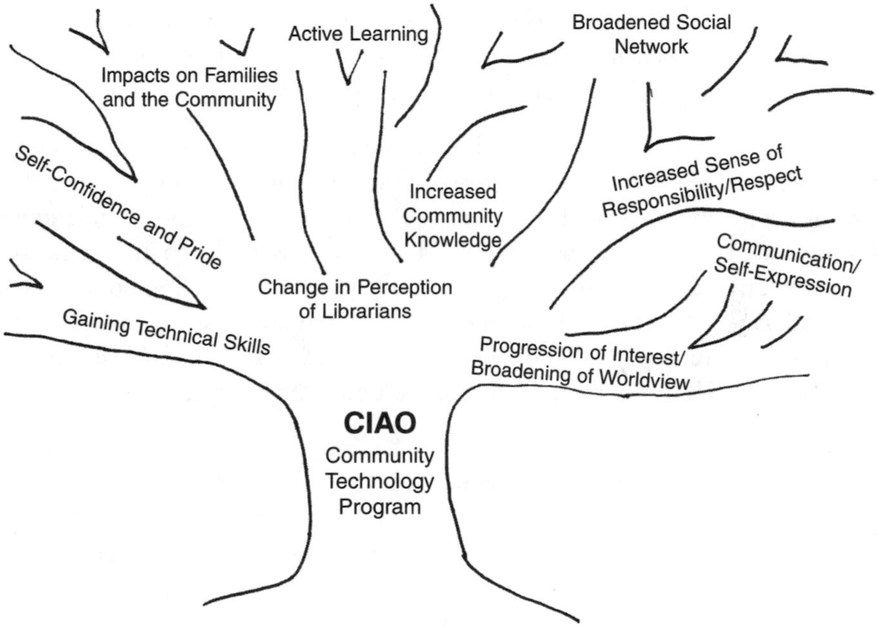

Active Learning

Broadened Social Network

Impacts on Families and the Community

Self-Confidence and Pride

Increased Community Knowledge

Increased Sense of Responsibility/Respect

Communication/ Self-Expression

Change in Perception of Librarians

Gaining Technical Skills

Progression of Interest/ Broadening of Worldview

CIAO
Community Technology Program

organizations, it has helped me not just with the computers, but it has helped me get involved more than I was in my community. And now I can honestly say, oh, I have done this, or I have created web pages. Well, I've helped the neighborhood round table create their website, you know, by doing what I learned. Before the summer session I had never heard of Urban Gardens and that is a community program where they take kids within a community and they take a plot of land and they actually do gardens. The kids learn to work with each other and they learn to work with things in their communities and they learn to work with their hands and things. I had never heard of that before; and I heard about that and it's kind of like, okay there is another good something in Flint that's going on.

Building on the previous gains, it appears that *some participants became more actively engaged.*

If you would speak to my mother she would probably say thank God for the CIAO program, because ever since I've been involved with it I guess you could say I've taken on a new direction. Like I said I've gotten more community involved and I work with little kids better and I worked with people better than I did before I got into the program. Um, I know she likes the program. Her and Cynthia and Leslie, they've gotten to know each other and it's kind of like, well, if K __ __ wasn't doing this, what would she be doing now type thing. So I know she's really thankful I've gotten involved with the CIAO program. (Teen coach)

CIAO staff and participants both noted *changes in participant perceptions and attitudes.* Leaders noticed youths' increasing trust in staff and graduate student coaches. The ability to trust is a precursor to the ability to develop relationships. Teens shared stories and aspirations with librarians and coaches. One of the teenagers arrived at the final program session wearing her high school graduation cap and gown, indicating how much she valued the respect of the staff and coaches. Participants, in addition, developed a *sense of responsibility* for their work and *showed pride in their accomplishments.* One participant commented:

> I felt like there was a job for me to do and I did it. And we're getting rewarded for it by what we learned. [With other things I have done] I felt like that was something I was just doing and it didn't mean anything to me then; if I was just sleeping and I missed it I would be like "oh well" and just kept on going about my business. But I felt that I got up, I came, and that's a big responsibility that you gotta learn to do. That it's a job for you to do and you gotta do it.

Participants and staff noted changes in their *social behavior and building social capital.* These changes could be seen in new social patterns of engagement, relationship building, and expanding social networks. Participants valued the networks of librarians in the community, as seen in the comments of one participant, "Um . . . [I enjoyed] especially working with [name of librarian], she knows so many people." These connections provided new participants, and the fact that students were associated with the library opened doors that were generally closed to teenagers.

Finally, we identified a group of *family and community outcomes* that extended beyond the teens to their families and neighborhoods. Participants shared their knowledge with their families, teachers, and others in the community. Their activities, as a result, produced outcomes that are more difficult to measure, but no less real. A story shared by one of the participants, "Jane," illustrates the value of the program to her family. An adult friend of hers saw a local news report on the celebration marking the completion of the CIAO web projects, and called the family to offer congratulations. The next day her mother made the significant investment of buying a computer. "This week has been crazy," Jane told the librarians, "every five minutes it's 'Jane! Come help your mother' and I have to go open up

Word for her or something." Jane plans to build a website for the family business using the new computer. What really impressed one of the graduate student coaches was that the program made it possible "for one of our students to literally burst through the digital divide . . . [and take] her entire family with her."

The candidate outcomes of the CIAO program are shown in figure 10-4, along with the activities and inputs that generated them.

Figure 10-4 Candidate Outcomes of the
Flint Public Library's CIAO Program*

Outcome: Gaining Technical Skills	Activities That Foster Technical Skill Development	Inputs That Foster Technical Skill Development**
Participants gained technical skills, such as learning how to use a computer	Hands-on instruction	A computer lab with one computer per participant
Learned how to use selected software products	Followed a creative and detailed curriculum	Internet access
Evaluated the quality of Internet resources	Encouraged participants to use technology to express themselves	Software, including website development tools: Adobe Photoshop, MS FrontPage
Learned how to create a website	Emphasized project-based learning	Digital cameras
Learned how to use a digital camera	Used humor to teach technology concepts	Staff with technical skills
Used Photoshop to create their own digital art	Created games to teach technology concepts	Staff with instructional skills
Learned how to use scanner and Import scanned images into a web page		
Learned about various useful and interesting websites		
Students gained skill in using software programs that became the basis for information exchange among participants		

* Outcomes in the first column are the result of activities and inputs in columns 2 and 3.
** Some of the inputs in column 3 are consistent and won't be repeated for the sake of brevity.

(continued)

Figure 10-4 *(continued)*

Outcome: Communication/ Self-Expression Gains	Activities That Foster Communication/ Self-Expression Gains	Inputs That Foster Communication/ Self-Expression Gains
Participants noted a change in their ability to communicate easily with strangers Participants improved their writing skills Participants worked collaboratively Teen coaches honed their teaching and coaching skills as well	Activities/strategies that foster active learning and team development such as: Fostering joint development of a project Creating a mentoring relationship with youth Informal teaching style	Staff with strong communication skills Staff with a commitment to develop communication and self-expression skills in teens A room that fosters communication Time for staff and kids to interact
Outcome: Active Learning Gains	**Activities That Foster Active Learning Gains**	**Inputs That Foster Active Learning Gains**
Students teamed up, learned things together, shared their knowledge with others Participants learned to draw on each other's strengths Participants' learning was reinforced	Involve students with the project Students with skills from past program given authority to act as assistant teachers Staff encourage students to teach each other Assign small groups Students are taught to teach others	"Coaching" staff Teen mentors Time reserved for students to experiment, communicate with each other A room that fosters communication
Outcome: Increased Community Knowledge	**Activities That Foster Increased Community Knowledge**	**Inputs That Foster Increased Community Knowledge**
Increased participant knowledge of the community Increased pride in the community Increased community involvement	Discussion about the community fostered among students The opportunity to meet community group leaders Gaining knowledge of the community encouraged Staff share their community contacts with participants Assignment involving working with a specific community organization Researching community organization or other aspect of the community	Staff that are knowledgeable about the community Access to the community through transportation, telephone, e-mail Library community resources Librarians

Outcome: Progression of Interest/ Broadening of Worldview	Activities That Foster Progression of Interest/ Broadening of Worldview	Inputs That Foster Progression of Interest/ Broadening of Worldview
Participants experience heightened awareness of self, community Awareness of new career options Improved ability to relate to adults, community	Staff shares experiences, information about adult life, career options, the community	Staff with teaching ability, broad worldview Computer lab with Internet access Time for casual conversation between staff and participants A room that fosters communication
Outcome: Change in Perception of Librarians	**Activities That Foster Change in Perception of Librarians**	**Inputs That Foster Change in Perception of Librarians**
Perception of librarian as trusted adult Participants want to make the librarians proud of them	Willingness to spend time with participant and family Providing transportation home and around community Expressing interest in participants' lives and activities	Librarians who do not fit participants' previous stereotyped image Time allotted to staff to devote to kids Welcoming, friendly staff
Outcome: Self-Confidence and Pride	**Activities That Foster Self-Confidence and Pride**	**Inputs That Foster Self-Confidence and Pride**
Gains in self-confidence and pride A shift in peer attitudes and respect	Completing a long-term web project with attainable goals Celebrating participants' achievements Completing small tasks on the computer with attainable goals Bringing in television crew to film final celebration	Staff that focus on kids Periodic celebrations with food Computer lab, easy-to-use software Time for staff and kids to interact
Outcome: Increased Sense of Responsibility/Respect	**Activities That Foster Increased Sense of Responsibility/Respect**	**Inputs That Foster Increased Sense of Responsibility/Respect**
Increased sense of responsibility/respect Assumption of responsibility Participants overcame difficulties in order to attend "work"	A common understanding among librarians, coaches, and participants that CIAO was a job Participants signed in and out of each CIAO session	Funding to pay participants for their work Welcoming, friendly staff Time for staff and kids to interact

(continued)

Figure 10-4   (*continued*)

Outcome: Broadened Social Network	Activities That Foster Broadened Social Network	Inputs That Foster Broadened Social Network
Ability to build social capital in the community A lasting impression that affects the willingness of youth to form trusting relationships with adults Participants access the networks of the librarians in the community Strengthening the teens' own personal networks	Willingness to share their personal community connections with participants Providing transportation around community Assigning participants collaborative activities Informal environment	Staff with strong community networks A room that fosters communication
Outcome: Impacts on Families and the Community	**Activities/Strategies for Impacts on Families and the Community**	**Inputs That Foster Impacts on Families and the Community**
Family buys computer, uses it to start home business Family, teachers, friends of participants gain technology skills Community organizations gain a web presence Participants volunteer in community after the project has ended	Participants share their knowledge with their families, teachers, and others in the community Providing transportation around community Project requires teens to research and create a community website	Goal of fostering civic engagement among teens Welcoming, friendly staff Perception of library as safe place Computer lab with Internet access Time for staff to interact with families and kids

Haines Outcomes

Through its outcome evaluation, the Haines Public Library learned that for mentors and mentees alike, participation in the Dragonfly Project resulted in a positive, even transforming experience that provided them with new skills and new connections to the community.

According to the evaluators, Dragonfly mentors have blossomed, gaining greater confidence and a greater willingness to share their skills with peers and adults. In addition to *their gains in technology skills*, which ranged from learning successful Internet searching strategies to desktop publishing and using the library's OPAC, mentors also learned to be more patient, tolerant, and kind when working with mentees and other people needing assistance. As a result, *mentors have not only gained, but refined, their teaching skills and their interpersonal skills as well.* Mentors' skill development also *encompasses improved writing and prob-*

lem-solving skills and, for some, enhanced academic performance. In addition, mentors have reaped *job placement benefits*; for example, some of the mentors found summer employment, some became volunteers at the library or computer aides at the high school, and some have used their skills to help college classmates and nonprofit organizations. Through their participation, mentors have *gained increased pride and self-confidence and an increased sense of responsibility and respect.* Most report that they feel more confident and more comfortable when interacting with adults and peers, more confident in pursuing their dreams, and, powerfully, they realize that their knowledge brings respect.

Mentees, too, *gained more confidence,* tackling skills that were foreign and fearsome to them. Many of the respondents noted *changes in their perceptions of technology and young people.* They feel more at ease with young people and with using computers and are *now using the technology skills they have developed for personal and work-related tasks.* For example, respondents report using e-mail to communicate and the Internet to do research, shop, send photographs, purchase airline tickets, and pay bills. Other mentees increased their skills in certain programs, especially Microsoft Excel, and applied them at work or at their business. Most have become advocates of the program and share their experiences with other community members, resulting in *positive awareness of the program.*

The Dragonfly Project has indeed become, as its symbol suggests, transformative. A greater number of the Haines community now *see the library as more than just a place to check out books; they see it as a place that is responsive to their needs, a place that is safe and committed to helping people of all ages in the community.* Given that the Dragonfly Project received funding from the borough for another year, it is apparently seen as a valuable resource, a program that provides free computer instruction given by people who are approachable, accessible, and respectful. The program is also seen as helping young people utilize their talents in a productive way and helping them transition into the work world.

The evaluation outcomes of the Dragonfly Project are shown in figure 10-5, along with the activities and inputs that generated them.

Collectively the youth programs discussed in this chapter provide what participants consider a safe and welcoming place—often a rarity in the communities that these programs serve. As seen in the tables of outcome in this chapter, the programs give students, and through them, their communities, technology skills and knowledge that they can and do use. They contribute to a range of personal, social, and communication skills for participants and at times for their families. These programs broaden the worldviews of the youth who participate and the adults who surround them. They foster active learning gains and skills and, for some, increased civic engagement and social capital gains.

Figure 10-5   Evaluation Outcomes for the Haines Dragonfly Project

Outcome: Computer Skills Acquired by Mentees	Activities Used to Teach Skills	Equipment and Personnel Needed to Acquire Skills
Learned basic computer terms and usage	Hands-on learning Technology awareness classes One-on-one mentoring	Laptop computers with Internet access, printer, LCD projector, screen Education and technology coordinators, mentors Conclusive environment Curriculum
Learned selected software programs	Hands-on learning Technology awareness classes One-on-one mentoring	Same as above, with software programs Microsoft Word, Access, Excel, Publisher, PowerPoint, Adobe Photoshop Elements, Macromedia Dreamweaver E-mail, Internet access
Learned how to search the Internet to get results and evaluate site quality	Hands-on learning Technology awareness classes One-on-one mentoring	Same as above Brochure on searching the Internet and SLED
Learned how to use a scanner	Hands-on learning; scan personal photo	Scanner Mentor
Learned library's online catalog	Hands-on learning Technology awareness classes One-on-one mentoring	Same as box 1
Outcome: Skills Used for Personal and Work-Related Tasks	**Activities That Foster Acquired Skills**	**Equipment and Personnel Needed to Acquire Skills**
E-mail family, friends, and use of business	Applying skills learned from class and mentoring sessions on e-mail	Staff, mentors, computer equipment, Internet access
Set up spreadsheets for business and personal use	Work with mentors one-on-one to create spreadsheets for particular personal and work-related tasks	Mentors Laptop computers with software programs and Internet access Conducive environment

Outcome: Skills Used for Personal and Work-Related Tasks	Activities That Foster Acquired Skills	Equipment and Personnel Needed to Acquire Skills
Greater proficiency with Microsoft Excel	Participated in an Excel Q&A night where participants asked how to do specific tasks and applied them at work/home	Mentors Laptop computers with software programs and Internet access LCD projector Conducive environment
Create greeting cards, flyers, brochures, business cards, letterhead, programs, and other printed materials	Applying skills learned from class on Microsoft Publisher or mentoring session on home computer or using library's computer equipment	Computer equipment Printer
Edited and manipulated photographs	Work with mentors one-on-one Use skills at home on personal equipment or using library's computer equipment	Mentor to guide process Computer, scanner Publisher and Photoshop Elements
Created resumes, cover letters	Work with mentors one-on-one Use skills learned in class or from one-on-one mentoring on personal equipment at home or using library's computer equipment	Mentor Computer equipment and Microsoft Publisher Printer
Created PowerPoint presentations of family photos, historical community photos, and for business	Work with mentors one-on-one Use skills learned in class or from one-on-one mentoring on personal equipment at home or using library's equipment	Mentor Computer equipment and Microsoft PowerPoint
Searched the Internet to do research, find jobs, check stock prices, shop, and locate items	Hands-on learning at library; applying skills learned in class or mentoring session at home	Mentor Computer equipment Internet access
Used library's online catalog more proficiently	Accessing library's catalog in library and remotely E-mailing requests and renewals of materials	Computer Internet access

(continued)

Figure 10-5   *(continued)*

Created database of family recipes	Applying skills learned in class teaching Microsoft Access	Computer, Microsoft Access Staff, mentors LCD projector
Volunteered to set up contact database for nonprofit organizations	Applying skills learned from class on Microsoft Access or from mentoring session	Mentor Computer equipment, Microsoft Access
Outcome: Improved Interpersonal Skills	**Activities That Helped Develop Interpersonal Skills**	**Equipment and Personnel Needed to Develop Interpersonal Skills**
More ease and confidence interacting with young people and others in community	Participating in technology awareness classes and signing up for one-on-one mentoring sessions	Mentors, conducive environment, computer equipment
Outcome: Improved Thinking/ Problem-Solving Skills	**Activities That Helped Develop Thinking Skills**	**Equipment and Personnel Needed to Develop Thinking Skills**
Confidence figuring out answers to technology questions	Watching education and technology coordinators, mentors, and others solve problems Asking questions of others Learning how to use office assistant, manuals, and online resources	Staff and computer with Internet access
Outcome: Change in Perception of Young People	**Activities That Aided Change in Perception**	**Equipment and Personnel Needed**
Mentees ask young people to help them	Working with young people in class and one-on-one	Mentors, computers, conducive environment
Mentees see young people making valuable contributions to the community	Seeing young people volunteer their time to help community members of all ages Good press Program receiving national/ state awards for excellence	Mentors, computers, conducive environment Library director applying for awards
Outcome: Change in Perception of Library and Librarians	**Activities That Aided Change in Perception**	**Equipment and Personnel Needed**
Library seen as more than a place to check out books and do research	Offering free access to computer equipment and computer learning classes One-on-one mentoring	Computers, software, staff, mentors

Outcome: Pride and Self-Confidence	Activities That Aided Change	Equipment and Personnel Needed
Mentees gained new skills they once feared	Attending classes and one-on-one mentoring sessions and creating products such as cards, spread-sheets, databases, etc.	Computers, software, mentors, staff, conducive environment
Mentees promote program to others in community	Word of mouth, bringing others to class or for mentoring session	
Outcome: Increased Interaction or Communication with Coworkers and Family	Activities That Aided Change	Equipment and Personnel Needed
Mentees shared skills with family, friends, and coworkers	Learning new computer skills in class or in mentoring session and sharing them at home and at work	Computers, software programs, staff, mentors
Technology is used to communicate with friends, family, and others remotely	Learning e-mail and sharing skill with parents, grand-parents, friends, and other family members	Computers, software program, Internet access
Outcome: Positive Awareness of Program	Activities That Provided Awareness	Equipment and Personnel Needed
Mentees tell others that staff and mentors are approachable, accessible, and friendly	Hands-on learning and creating curriculum that uses community interests to teach basic skills	Staff, mentors, computer equipment, conducive environment
Entire community sees program as a positive force for engaging youth and elders	Good press, TV news spot, radio publicity, PSAs, word of mouth, visits to organizations/schools, flyers	Staff that are familiar with public relations techniques
Community sees program as valuable service worth funding. (Program received funding from borough for additional year.)	Cumulation of all activities	
Program continues to attract new mentees and mentors	Cumulation of all activities	

Chapter 11

Strengthening Community

Outcomes of Community Information Services

The Community Information Program (CIP) of the Peninsula Library System (PLS) of San Mateo County, California, believes that "the library is in the business of data collection." While the CIP itself is not a direct service provider, its role is to provide accurate and up-to-date information to agencies that provide direct services. Its clientele include the social service agencies and library staff that use the CIP database, or that use the many specialized publications produced by the CIP. Using a variety of strategies, the CIP generates myriad outcomes for local service providers, and through them, the San Mateo County community at large. A pioneer in its field, succeeding through two decades of operation, the CIP program demonstrates the range of outcomes that librarians can expect from an information and referral service that has become an integral and leading component of the community it serves.

The CIP's Model, Strategies, and Professional Contributions

Over its twenty-five-year evolution, the Community Information Program has developed an information model around a scheme of strategies involving the database, information sharing and networking, and community leadership designed to facilitate the provision of community information. More important, the combined execution of these strategies has positioned the CIP as an initiator of a diverse range of outcomes that show how it helps the human services community and through them the citizens of San Mateo County.

Community Information Database Activities

Started in 1974, the CIP was one of the first library-based interactive information and referral services in the United States. The CIP database of community information was originally developed using the Stanford Public Information and Retrieval System. The database was housed on the Stanford mainframe, and librarians accessed it through teletype machines connected through the sheriff's microwave system. In 1998 the CIP transferred its database from the Stanford mainframe to a Microsoft Access database located on the county network. With current Internet technology, the CIP has also put the database into a searchable flat-text file on the Peninsula Library System's website.

The database serves as the root from which all other strategies and outcomes grow. CIP staff update the database through a variety of feedback mechanisms to ensure that it remains the most up-to-date and reliable source for community information in the county. The CIP's active database management in turn supports its well developed client-based services.

CIP staff leverage the database to create value-added products that aid communication and decision making in the community. From the database the CIP generates mailing labels on demand that allow community agencies and organizations to target clients. In addition, the CIP publishes a biennial directory of community organizations that now encompasses contact details and descriptions of over 3,000 organizations and three indices of the most utilized services in the area. At the same time, the CIP collaborates with community organizations to identify the need for and then develop specialized information resource guides from its database, such as *How to Handle a Rental Dispute, Food Resources in San Mateo County, Youth Services Directory for San Mateo County, Help at Home, Survival in San Mateo County—A Street Guide to Emergency Resources* (available in English and Spanish), and more. These guides are translated into other languages as appropriate and include icons designed to reach illiterate and non-English speaking populations.

The CIP develops value-added products that aid community decision making, notably statistical and mapping outputs. The CIP's statistics service supports data collection and analysis of individual constituencies, such as the disability community, and compiles budget and staffing information on county nonprofit organizations. The CIP's mapping service creates custom maps that visualize data, including visual representations of demographic spreads and community needs assessments that can assist agencies and nonprofits in their grant and decision-making activities.

Information-Sharing and Networking Activities

The CIP's well-honed strategies and activities produce a powerful set of varying but incremental outcomes for the citizens of San Mateo County by strengthening its governmental and nonprofit social services providers. The CIP employs a range of information-sharing and networking strategies, including a monthly orientation to community services, meetings and training for service providers, and a quarterly bulletin (also available online) that identifies new and changing resources in the county. These products and services build upon the CIP's database and staff expertise. Every month the CIP hosts an orientation that draws new agency and nonprofit staff from across the county. During orientation, CIP staff introduce the program's resources and services and thus enhance both the ability of their audience to access relevant and reliable information and the effectiveness of the CIP itself. Participants benefit from the opportunity to "meet and greet" members of other community agencies and organizations represented at the orientation. Knowledge of and access to such community resources helps community organizations to respond more effectively to their constituencies. Broadly speaking, the orientation event mobilizes community organizations as information providers while it also helps them to recognize the value of the library system's knowledge and values. These sessions, usually attended by nonprofit agency staff, school counselors, hospital information and referral workers, and other area professionals, play an essential role in introducing service providers to both the community information resources of the CIP and to each other. In San Mateo County, such meetings have become a forum for building relationships wherein service providers plant the seeds for future cooperation and collaboration with each other.

To further cultivate these community relationships and in turn propagate information sharing among community actors, the CIP coordinates monthly inter-agency forums for providers. Provider meetings focus on particular themes, such as care for seniors, and take place in a variety of locations across the county. As a mechanism to support routine exposure to community organizations and activities, these provider meetings enable information sharing and networking. Community information then continues to diffuse throughout the community as attendees return to their native organizations and share information with colleagues.

In recognition of the time and resource limitations that meetings can pose, the CIP has developed a third strategy to broaden the dissemination of community information: distribution of the CIP's quarterly newsletter, the *Resource Bulletin*. Mailed to 3,600 recipients, the newsletter includes CIP activities, updates to its database and to its 600-page *Directory of Human Services*, and new agency-sponsored programs. The spirit of the newsletter is dedicated to information sharing for the community at large. According to a CIP staff member, "[the *Resource Bulletin*] is not about us, it's about the county service agencies and the nonprofit agencies and what they are doing."

Community Positioning and Leadership Activities

The CIP often acts a key collaborator with many community organizations. Several projects have resulted from these collaborative relationships built up over a period of time. For example, the core products of the CIP's publishing program, such as CIP directories, *Help at Home*, and *Survival in San Mateo County—A Street Guide to Emergency Resources*, originated as requests from county services agencies. The CIP's partnership with the Health Services Agency (HSA) has led the CIP to maintain a database of residential care homes in the county; in addition, the CIP has collaborated with the HSA to streamline the development of the New Beginning Coalition, a service for older adults and adults with disabilities, with full community buy-in. According to HSA staff, "[the CIP was] instrumental in helping us to organize in such a way that we could ensure that there was buy-in from all the various constituencies."

Over time, based on the credibility it has earned through its top-notch information service (as well as its impartiality) and the visibility it has gained through its role as a primary actor in community development, the CIP has emerged as a leader among service providers in San Mateo County. The statement of one agency director aptly captures many aspects of the CIP's valued role in the community: "Everybody knows the CIP. They have a strong institutional history and are a really tremendous resource in many different ways."

Professional Contributions

The CIP accomplishes this impressive range of activities with a small but talented staff. Over her thirty-year tenure, Janet Hofman (now retired) guided the CIP to the position of leadership it now enjoys. As noted previously, the CIP provides visibility for both itself and the Peninsula Library System among the social services agencies of county government, the related nonprofit community, and the foundation community. CIP staff also conduct presentations at city council meetings. As a result of its legacy of coordination, collaboration, and capacity building among service providers in San Mateo County, today a number of clients consider CIP a partner organization. In the words of one customer, "Janet is so highly regarded throughout the entire community. Her commitment to the community is so great . . . she always goes the extra mile . . . the staff that she brings on board are the same kind of people, they go the extra mile."

The CIP's remaining staff complement the CIP leadership with their commitment, their technical expertise, and their knowledge of the community and its needs. The staff update and manage the CIP's core asset, its database.

The CIP's Clientele

Located outside of San Francisco, San Mateo County is home to a population that is both affluent and diverse. With more than 700,000 residents, the county has a median household income of $70,819. The census shows that 60 percent of residents are white, 20 percent are Asian, 22 percent are Hispanic, and 3 percent are black.

The CIP itself is not a direct service provider; its role is to provide accurate and up-to-date information to agencies that provide direct service. In the words of one CIP staff member, "We get information out to the providers and the providers get it out to the community." The CIP's clientele includes the social service agencies and library staff that use the database, or that use the many specialized publications produced by the CIP on their behalf. In pursuit and advancement of their professional goals, these service providers need, among other requisites, reliable information and knowledge about the community; organizational efficiency; outreach capability; partnership opportunities; and continuous grant development.

Indicators of the Impact of the CIP

We have grouped the outcomes of the Community Information Program into six categories of impact, as shown in figure 11-1. The first three show that the CIP acts to *increase community knowledge* and *foster information sharing*, which leads to increased communication; building on the first two, the CIP *facilitates coordination and collaboration*. The benefits cumulate further, and the CIP appears to help *build capacity* among community organizations. These more effective organizations note that this service contributes to *improved delivery of agency services*.

Figure 11-1 Community Information Program Outcomes
for Human Service Organizations

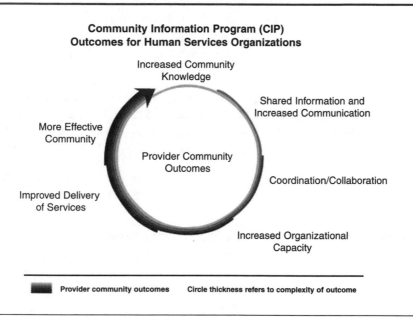

**Community Information Program (CIP)
Outcomes for Human Services Organizations**

Increased Community
Knowledge

Shared Information and
Increased Communication

More Effective
Community

Provider Community
Outcomes

Coordination/Collaboration

Improved Delivery
of Services

Increased Organizational
Capacity

■ **Provider community outcomes** 　 **Circle thickness refers to complexity of outcome**

Collectively, these changes result in a *more effective community,* which in turn leads to increases in community knowledge, and thus perpetuates the cycle of outcomes that assist the provider community and the citizens of San Mateo County.

In the process, and as a result of its long history, experience, and effectiveness, the CIP has earned broad praise and respect:

Everybody knows the CIP. They have a strong institutional history and are a really tremendous resource in many different ways. (Agency director)

CIP know what they are doing. (Agency director)

They are a good crew . . . You have seen for yourself what a real service they provide. It is a real tight, progressive organization. (Direct service provider)

The six categories of outcomes achieved by the CIP are described in the sections that follow.

Increased Community Knowledge

Agencies value their increased knowledge of the community that results from the effective management of the CIP database. Agencies additionally appreciate the CIP's directory, guides, and quarterly updates as a major information resource about the community, and have come to recognize the CIP as a provider of up-to-date and reliable information.

> When [we] do a presentation to the city of San Mateo and I want to know some very specific information about the city of San Mateo, that is when I turn to CIP . . . They are also the repository for . . . darn near every report that anyone's ever written about anything . . . that's a great resource. (Agency director)

> You really count on CIP and current information . . . They keep so current on everything that it is a pleasure. (Direct service provider)

Shared Information and Increased Communication

Information sharing and its corollary, increased communication among organizations, are fostered through a variety of CIP outreach mechanisms. For example, agencies use mailing labels generated by the CIP database to increase communication with relevant audiences. New agency staff learn to use community information resources through CIP orientations, and encourage others to do the same. At CIP meetings and through its publications, agencies regularly share information not only about community problems, but also about the contributions of service organizations to their solution. In addition, agencies publish information about themselves and learn about changes in other agencies through the CIP's quarterly newsletter, *Resource Bulletin*, which reinforces information sharing and communication throughout the provider community of 3,600 recipients. Says one service provider, "Their newsletter is marvelous because it keeps you up-to-date with all of the new things that are available to our clients and staff. And that's worth its weight in gold."

> We got our learning . . . from CIP training. Whenever I hire somebody new, whenever I am in a collaborative that hires somebody new, I give them the CIP phone number to call them for an . . . orientation to the resources in the county. And you can see the difference. (Agency director)

> Different service providers throughout San Mateo County come together on a bimonthly basis, and the CIP is instrumental in helping to ensure that that is continuing to happen in our county. (Agency director)

Coordination and Collaboration

Agencies recognize that the CIP facilitates connections, responsiveness, and synergies within the provider community. San Mateo agencies identify the need for appropriate specialized information resources and then work with the CIP to develop them (e.g., *Survival Guide* for the homeless, *Help at Home* for aging populations, *How to Handle a Rental Dispute*, etc.). These partnerships lead to

- the identification of new resources
- new contacts
- the production of relevant specialized resource directories

As a result, agencies feel empowered by their increased connections with other agencies fostered by the CIP through bimonthly interagency forums. CIP staff attend provider meetings and maintain the mailing lists and flyers for meetings.

Of key importance, agencies trust the CIP as an organization that anticipates community needs, one that can identify and respond to opportunities across the provider community. Agencies recognize the CIP's leadership in fostering community collaboration and count on it to keep them connected with issues and with other groups. The CIP's community positioning and leadership—built on its credibility and visibility—help it to spearhead collaboration among community organizations in response to emerging and existent community needs.

> We'll go to the Community Information Program . . . and contract with them to help us develop a system for identifying vacancies in the board and care communities . . . They have the skills to develop that database and maintain it for us. (Agency director)

> When I need to contact somebody about a resource, it's a direct contact. We've talked; we know who we are. It's very, very helpful to have that personal contact at the provider meetings . . . at the CIP orientation, and you will also meet key people in the field of social services and nonprofit organizations. So, this is a must; and people come back saying wow! (Agency director)

> [Janet] sees a need and works to build a response to it. For example, some time ago Janet worked to build collaborations around the landlord-tenant issue. It took a lot of meetings, but was developed. (Agency director)

> We count on [Janet] and her folks in the library system to keep us connected to other issues and stuff. I mean she sits on planning groups for a lot of different organizations . . . and she'll bring those issues and people to my attention and link

us together. But she'll keep us connected to some of the other issues . . . you can integrate to the extent that you have the ability to ebb and flow around the different other committees. And we look to [Janet] to bring the critical issues to us. (Agency director)

Capacity Building

The capacity and effectiveness of county social service agencies and organizations are increased through the CIP's efficiencies. The CIP saves time for county agencies and organizations through its database and publications strategies, and it is recognized as a "one-stop shopping" agency that reduces duplication of effort by serving as a hub for community information. Social services agencies say their decision making is enhanced with custom-developed CIP statistics as well as monthly charts and graphs developed for agency use. Likewise, social services agencies and nonprofits say the CIP supports their decision- and grant-making activities by the creation of relevant special-purpose maps that visualize data. CIP maps display the distribution of clients and services throughout the county, and decision makers analyze these maps to corroborate or modify county policies and practices. As one agency director put it, "CIP helps assure that we don't reinvent the wheel. CIP knows the information about the community; we don't need to know it too. We can go to CIP."

> When it comes to disabilities, people either don't identify [them] or there are a million definitions, and we ask CIP to help us organize statistical information related to disability. To identify the various groups that collect it and put it together into one binder . . . at least we have a start at addressing the issue of who we are really talking about here because all of our grants and everything else is based on some sort of prevalence . . . And we have done some significant program development based on a lot of the information that CIP helps us with.

> The AIDS Program of the San Mateo County Health Service Agency came to us for a map showing where the AIDS cases were in the county . . . the majority were in a specific part of the county and so the director took it to the staff and said "see, well of course it's going to be much easier for them to go to a clinic closer to home" . . . it backed up a policy by the administration to the staff to prove that this was the right thing to do. (CIP staff)

> We have done some significant program development based on a lot of the information that CIP developed: the maps that showed where the cluster of welfare participants lived in the county, and at other times to show where the poverty

pockets were in the county, which were very helpful in writing grants and proposals for additional child-care subsidies and also capacity building for where the
new facility is needed. And the maps clearly demonstrated to the county of San
Mateo, the county welfare department Human Services Agency, and to our
agency where we needed to work on developing child-care homes and centers.
(Agency director)

Improved Delivery of Agency Services

Social services agencies and organizations improve their delivery of services to
their client base through the extensive support they receive from the CIP.
Agencies and organizations find new or different clients by using the CIP's mailing list service and resource guides. County agencies reach out to other community organizations to improve services to constituencies by using the CIP's mailing
label services. Agencies are able to disseminate information to potential clientele
through the CIP, as well as to match clients with services and foster the self-suffi-
ciency of their client base through CIP resources.

> That [labels] really generated a client base for us where we were not only educat-
> ing the community about the program, but also recruiting clients. (Direct service
> provider)

> [Janet] introduced us to . . . the larger library system, whereby we utilized that as
> a method of disseminating information. Say it's child abuse awareness month and
> we have 10,000 brochures . . . we can come and put them here and they'll get
> them all out there. That's incredible distribution. (Agency director)

> [The CIP directory] gives people options. It gives them places to go and people
> to refer to. One leads to another, leads to another as people really become
> informed . . . we make it our business to inform them. Because this is such an
> incredible resource, that they really do need to have it in their hands, which is
> why we hand it out at our desk.

> CIP puts out a brochure called *Help for the Homeless in San Mateo County*. A
> lot of people have access to that. It is given out in a lot of different places. The
> booklet has icons that show house or food to help people figure out what they can
> get in case they can't read and they can figure it out from the pictures. After a per-
> son leaves our office after a first visit, we will have begun to help them in the ways
> we can, and then depending on what it was, we follow up with them, asking them
> "did you call legal aid," or "did you go down to family law services like you
> planned on doing?" (Direct service provider)

More Effective Community

Based on the accumulation of the first five outcomes, the CIP acts as a major contributor to community development in San Mateo County. By working together more effectively, community organizations begin to build a more effective community.

> [CIP's director] is the kind of person who is very good at community building, she's very good at asking questions of people to draw at information, it's one of her skills. She's really very good at putting people together and making bridges. (Agency director)

> We refer people through the contacts we've made through CIP, either just their directory or the meetings they sponsor throughout the county so that people connect, start a relationship, and it's so much easier to get services for your client if you've got a contact and they know you . . . so that really has precipitated better services to our clients over the years by the use of CIP.

> CIP is part of PLS. Until I sit down to write my contract every two years with Janet, I forget, as do most of us, that CIP isn't part of our department. They are so close . . . I have never had any kind of feeling like what we wanted to do we couldn't do with CIP . . . They are so much a part of us . . . The CIP client base . . . is all a family, this is all a big family. (Agency director)

The Peninsula Library System's Community Information Program has made a variety of positive impacts on the community. These outcomes are similar to ones identified in an earlier study which found that community networks can help overcome barriers, increase organizational effectiveness and responsiveness, increase the ability to access relevant information, mobilize community organizations as information providers, and contribute to community building.[1] It appears that the cycle of community outcomes discussed previously is the result of carefully crafted strategies. The reliable and up-to-date information provided by the CIP, as well as the connections that the program makes between community organizations, lead to larger outcomes. The six categories of outcomes, as seen by area human services organizations, start with the most basic—increasing the service providers' knowledge of the community—and ultimately reinforce the intrinsic value of community networks.

The candidate outcomes achieved by the CIP and the activities that generated them are shown in figure 11-2.

Figure 11-2   Service Activities and Candidate Outcomes of the Peninsula Library
System's Community Information Program*

Outcome: Increased Community Knowledge	Activities That Foster Increased Community Knowledge
CIP is seen as a provider of up-to-date and reliable information Agencies value CIP as a major information resource about the community	Publishes and distributes *Directory of Human Services* Develops knowledge of agency needs Develops and maintains database Produces maps that visualize community data Database-updating activities Custom-developed statistics as well as monthly charts and graphs Publishes and distributes specialized guides such as *Help at Home* and *Survival in San Mateo County—A Street Guide to Emergency Resources* Publishes and distributes quarterly updates, *Resource Bulletin*
Outcome: Shared Information and Increased Communication	Activities That Foster Shared Information and Increased Communication
Increased communication with relevant audiences New agency staff learn to use community information resources through CIP orientations, and encourage others to do the same Agencies publish information about themselves, and learn about changes in other agencies Agencies share information about the contributions of their organization to the solution of a community problem Regular information sharing and communication among agencies	CIP produces mailing labels which agencies request for specialized audiences Develops orientation packets for new agency staff Monthly orientation to community resources Makes broad connections in community High-profile leadership orientations conducted at agency requests CIP conducts monthly provider meetings, maintains the mailing lists, and produces flyers Publishes and distributes quarterly updates, resource proximity to the human service community bulletin

* Outcomes in the first column are the result of activities in column 2.   (*continued*)

Figure 11-2 *(continued)*

Outcome: Coordination and Collaboration	Activities That Foster Coordination and Collaboration
Agencies identify the need for appropriate specialized information resource guides and then work with CIP to develop them Agencies feel empowered by the increased connections among agencies Agencies trust CIP as an agency that anticipates community needs Community collaboration Visibility for CIP and PLS within the human services agencies of county government, in the related nonprofit community, and in the foundation community	CIP identifies and responds to opportunities across the provider community CIP conducts monthly provider meetings, maintains the mailing lists, and produces flyers Makes broad connections in community Publishes and distributes specialized guides such as *Help at Home* and *Survival in San Mateo County—A Street Guide to Emergency Resources* CIP staff conduct presentations at city council meetings CIP serves as a critical member in a number of collaboration partnerships that result in spinoff organizations CIP remains apolitical
Outcome: **Capacity Building**	**Activities That Foster** **Capacity Building**
County agencies and organizations save time Reduced duplication of effort Decision making is enhanced, supported Grant development activities are supported	CIP gets information out to the providers and the providers get it out to the community CIP produces mailing labels which agencies request for specialized audiences Provides one-stop shopping Custom-developed statistics as well as monthly charts and graphs Produces maps that visualize community data
Outcome: **Improved Delivery of Agency Services**	**Activities That Foster Improved** **Delivery of Agency Services**
Agencies and organizations find new or different clients Reaches out to other community organizations to improve services to constituencies Agencies are able disseminate information to potential clientele Matches clients with services and fosters the self-sufficiency of their client base	CIP produces mailing labels which agencies request for specialized audiences Regularly updates database Publishes and distributes specialized guides such as *Help at Home* and *Survival in San Mateo County—A Street Guide to Emergency Resources* Produces maps that visualize community data

Outcome: More Effective Community	Activities That Foster More Effective Community
More effective community	Maintaining the above activities, including investments in inputs

NOTE

1. J. C. Durrance and K. E. Pettigrew, "How Libraries and Librarians Help: Toward Context-Centered Methods for Evaluating Public Library Networked Community Information Initiatives," *First Monday* 6, no. 4 (April 2001), http://www.firstmonday.dk/.

Chapter 12

Putting the Pieces Together

An Outcome Study of the Ypsilanti District Library's Senior Deposit Collection Program

Dana Walker and Jeanie Fisher

Focusing on Seniors

One of the most profound demographic changes in the United States is that its population is getting older. In 2000 about one in every eight, or 35 million Americans, was age 65 or over. This represents a 12 percent increase since 1990. And these aging trends are expected to continue, especially as baby boomers enter the 65+ category. By the year 2030, it is anticipated that the older population will double to about 70 million adults. Furthermore, this population itself is getting older, with the 85+ population projected to increase from 4.2 million in 2000 to 8.9 million in 2030.[1]

Clearly, then, Americans are living longer. In addition, this aging population is increasingly educated, active, economically influential, and politically powerful. As the population continues to age it will demand new and different information resources and access to lifelong learning opportunities. It is here that the public library system has an opportunity, indeed, a responsibility, to shape programs and services that will meet the needs of the aging. As the American Library Association states in its "Library Services to Older Adults Guidelines," "It is essential for the leaders and policy makers of the library to understand that service for older adults is not a fad; the need and demand for library services will only increase."[2]

Unique Needs of the Aging Population

Although the ultimate goals of the public library—life enrichment, lifelong learning, and information access—are consistent for all library patrons, the older adult population has unique needs owing to the changes its members experience as they age. Celia Hales-Mabry groups these changes into physiological, psychological, and sociological ones.[3]

Physiological changes. Physiological changes can be significant for this population. Older adults are subject to more disabilities and see physicians about 50 percent more often than younger persons.[4] In addition, this population is more likely to experience losses in vision, hearing, and mobility. As such, reading or discussion may be difficult, and transportation (walking, driving, getting in and out of a car) may be challenging or impossible.

Psychological changes. Older adults experience psychological deficits such as memory loss or become subject to depression in response to major life transitions like widowhood or institutionalization.

Sociological changes. Finally, older adults experience significant sociological changes. Often they face a loss of their previous role as an active family or community member and thus feel a sense of marginalization. In addition, older adults may experience a reduction in their social and personal interactions which engenders feelings of isolation.

Enter the Public Library

The public library has played and will continue to play an important role as we see the effects of this dramatic demographic shift occurring. The library remains an accessible civic space for information provision and dissemination and lifelong learning. In the last several decades, a number of library programs and services focusing on the elderly have emerged. For example, extension services, such as books by mail, bookmobiles, deposit collections, and home delivery services, have become popular in many communities. Libraries have also dedicated significant special resources to seniors, including large-print and talking books. Some libraries have been active in providing senior-specific programming, including film and lecture series. Finally, special services—oral histories, bibliotherapy, and lifelong learning programs—have also gained popularity.[5]

Why an Outcome Evaluation?

Despite the plethora of programs focused on older adults, based on our own literature review, there seems to have been little evaluative work done on the effectiveness of these programs. Though there is an almost intuitive sense that senior outreach programs are valuable and worthwhile, even essential, there is a dearth of studies that explore how or why. The research that has been done, including the 1971 *National Survey of Public Library Services for Older Adults* conducted by Booz, Allen, and Hamilton and the 1985 follow-up by Betty Turock on that original survey, focused more on gathering information on extension services, special resources, group programs and special services for older adults.[6] In addition to these national surveys, a few smaller state surveys and reading interest surveys conducted for master's theses have been undertaken.[7]

However, this research has overwhelmingly been focused on quantitative output data—the types of programs available, how many are offered, the size of the older adult services staff, and collection statistics. To our knowledge, very little research has dealt with an outcome evaluation of library programming for older adults. It is our contention, then, that outcome studies such as the one discussed in this chapter are essential to truly understand what seniors want and need and how they benefit from the public library.

Studies like the *National Survey of Public Library Services for Older Adults* are important to understand the range of library programs available to the elderly. But these surveys serve almost as an inventory of what is available; they don't give researchers, librarians, or the general public a real understanding of how library programs are *benefiting* the senior population.

Arguably, then, the most important reason to conduct outcome-based evaluations in this area is to help determine how the programs have an impact on their users. It may be helpful to know that 100 people check out books from a deposit collection, but does that really help us know how a specific senior patron benefited from the availability of those books, or what impact the library and its programs are having on the patron's life? Probably not. What if instead of looking at the program and the data that surround it, we look at the patrons and the benefits they draw from the program? When we look at what users know, think, or can do differently after the program, we have a better understanding and evaluation of the service.[8] It is by looking at evaluation from this new vantage point—that of *user* benefits—that we are able to understand program *outcomes* from the perspective of senior patrons, not from the perspective of the library.

It was operating under this framework—looking at the seniors' own perceptions of the benefits gained from the senior deposit collection—that we undertook an outcome evaluation of the deposit program at the Ypsilanti (Mich.) District Library. The purpose of this chapter is to provide an understanding of the outcomes we uncovered during our two-month research process. We will start by providing a contextual background for understanding the Ypsilanti District Library's outreach program and its service model for the senior deposit collection. In addition, our study design and data collection strategies are detailed. The bulk of this chapter is dedicated to documenting the outcomes. Finally, we conclude with suggestions for further research or analysis.

Context: The Senior Deposit Collection Program

The Ypsilanti District Library

The Ypsilanti District Library (YDL) has been serving Ypsilanti, Michigan, and the surrounding townships for 135 years. By 1992 the library's user base had climbed to 70,000—far exceeding the main library's small 10,000-square-foot facility. That year, the library began an ambitious campaign to raise awareness of library services and needs, hoping to convince local politicians and taxpayers to approve the building of a new main library. In addition, it asked for city funds to renovate the former main library to become a downtown branch. The campaign succeeded, and in 2002 the new Ypsilanti District Library opened its doors to the public. The library staff now faced a new challenge: how to sustain and continue to build such community investment.

One way to do this is through outreach programming. The focus of the YDL's outreach programs is to serve the community while at the same time encouraging community members to join, visit, and use services available in the library. However, at the YDL there is no single operating unit for outreach. Each library department plans and implements its own outreach programming. The community relations coordinator works with library staff to help them develop connections and partnerships to support outreach initiatives in their departments.

Although the focus of this study is the Senior Deposit Collection Program at the YDL, it is important to note that the deposit program is only one part of a greater outreach emphasis at the library. The main outreach programs include the following ones.

Bookmobile. The bookmobile operates year-round and makes more than thirty stops throughout the Ypsilanti community. According to the YDL website, the bookmobile "serves as an alternative to stationary branches, and can go places where library use may otherwise be minimal or nonexistent."[9]

Books on Wheels. The Books on Wheels program is a free service to homebound library users, usually elderly, who are unable to visit the library in person.

Volunteers. The volunteers program brings community members into the library to help staff prepare for onsite programs, deliver books to homebound patrons, or greet patrons at the customer service desk.

Service Model: Senior Deposit Collection Program Operation

The senior deposit program's primary purpose is not to bring more patrons into the library or increase library membership. Instead, the deposit collection is targeted to older adults who are unable, or find it difficult, to visit the library in person. The service model is relatively straightforward. A library staff member, the community relations coordinator, organizes regular book deposits with subject-appropriate librarians who select books for nine senior centers and residential homes for the elderly in Ypsilanti. The deposit locations are varied, and each serves a different clientele with different needs. Seniors at the locations range in age, income, cognitive functioning, and level of independence and activity. The majority of these patrons are women, though men do constitute an important part of the patron demographic. These senior patrons may be in situations where they are living independently in a residential home, visiting a senior activity center, or in assisted living or nursing care and are benefiting from the books through planned activities, such as memory exercises.

The coordinator and adult services librarian deliver books to each deposit location every three months. The books, which are primarily for leisure reading and range from romance to historical novels, are selected by YDL adult services staff based on an understanding of location preferences and feedback from seniors.

In addition to being straightforward, the library's service model could be described as an informal support structure. The books are checked out through the library, but then the library leaves it up to each deposit location to manage circulation, use, and programming with the books. Feedback from seniors to the library staff is also informal, as some centers employ suggestion books while others try to catch the librarians during the drop-off.

Study Design

Determining Context

The Ypsilanti District Library does not have specific outcomes for the senior deposit collection program. Therefore, our first step was to gather ideas from a range of sources about what the outcomes are and what they should be. Without an understanding of our anticipated measurable outcomes, we couldn't effectively structure a study design. Before we could know what sorts of instruments to develop, what kinds of questions to ask, or even what sampling frame to select, we needed to learn more about the contextual factors relating to this study. Consequently, we spent much of our early work researching the background and broader context of the deposit program, both in terms of the program itself and the seniors it seeks to serve.

CONTEXT OF THE PROGRAM

In order to understand the broader context of the program, we began by interviewing the YDL library staff most directly involved in the senior deposit program: the community relations coordinator and two adult services librarians. The community relations coordinator is the central administrator for all outreach programs at the YDL, including the senior deposit program. From our interviews with her, we learned how the program fits within the larger context of the YDL and its outreach programs.

Two adult services librarians at the YDL are responsible for selecting materials for each participating drop-off location. It might be argued that the success of the program rests on a successful selection of books tailored for each center. Our interviews with both librarians gave us a better understanding of how books are selected and why, and in what ways the librarians have noticed the seniors responding to the collections.

CONTEXT OF THE USERS

We felt that an informed understanding of the population served by this program would play an important role in how we approached our study design. To this end, we conducted a literature search focused on other evaluative studies, as well as reports on a range of public library outreach programs to seniors. By reviewing this literature, we grew more familiar with the issues currently facing seniors and the issues faced by those organizations attempting to serve them. This information ultimately informed our project design and helped us identify measurable outcomes.

We became aware that we might have the best luck collecting data in person. We felt that making a personal connection with the seniors was important and therefore chose not to conduct any phone or written interviews. Based on our research, we believed that the social activity of visiting the seniors would have a greater impact than developing written surveys or feedback forms and hopefully would result in more valuable data. This decision to restrict our data collection methods did have the effect of reducing our sample size, however, since we knew we would not have time to do a large number of in-person interviews.

Based on our readings and early interviews, we also realized that this population presented some specific challenges. The physical limitations faced by many seniors (including hearing impairment that prevented phone interviews) meant that we needed to go to them. Even during in-person interviews with seniors such physical challenges were not absent. For example, during the course of this study we realized that some seniors found it physically uncomfortable to sit for any length of time during interviews. In fact, one woman had to leave after five minutes because her back was causing her too much pain. In addition, in one of our focus groups, one woman found it hard to participate because she could not hear the conversation. We found it challenging to draw her out for answers because she could not hear well. As a consequence, we had to adapt our process and not ask as many questions or ask them more slowly.

Originally, we planned to gather circulation statistics from each senior center's library to better understand how many residents were using the collection and to see if we could recognize any patterns. However, such statistics are independently maintained at each drop-off location, and we soon realized that the extent to which such circulation information is maintained varies greatly from center to center. We decided that this information was not reliable, and ultimately, did not inform the purposes of this study.

Sampling Frame Rationale

To include the staff and seniors at each one of the nine senior centers served by the program was beyond the scope of our case study. Therefore, we decided to focus specifically on residential senior homes and narrowed our sampling frame to two participating centers. We chose residential senior centers because they offer the advantage of a "captive audience"—the patrons live where the books are used, which makes it easier (both for them and for us) to conduct interviews, focus groups, and observations. Also, there tends to be more extensive programming in residential homes versus nonresidential centers.

We selected our two sample centers based on the recommendation of the YDL community relations coordinator. This did introduce a certain level of bias into our sample since our selection was not random. However, we felt our main goal was to determine program outcomes; thus, we reasoned that our best chance of uncovering measurable outcomes was to find particularly active and approachable participating centers.

Because the purpose of our report was to unearth outcomes that show how the program benefits those it intends to serve, we focused the bulk of our data collection on a sampling of seniors at each of the two residential centers. We felt it was important to hear from the seniors on how they perceived the program—how they used the library, what kind of impact it had on their situation, and if they noticed any areas for improvement.

In addition to interviewing a sampling of seniors at each one of the two residential centers, we felt it was important to interview the activity directors at the centers. The activity directors at each participating senior center determine the extent to which YDL books are incorporated into their center's programming and therefore spend the greatest amount of time experiencing the benefits of the deposit program. Interviewing the activity directors ensured that our sampling frame would include those working directly with the patrons who use materials provided by the program (since the YDL librarians didn't necessarily have direct contact with the patrons).

Instrument Development

Based on the contextual factors just described, we developed our data collection instruments to encourage stories, reflection, and discussion. We created four interview scripts—one with general questions, one for the community relations director, one for the YDL adult services librarians, and one for activity directors. We also created a list of questions that we used to conduct focus groups. We tested these instruments as we used them and modified them when appropriate. The four data collection instruments are given below.

GENERAL INTERVIEW QUESTIONS

What is your involvement with the Senior Deposit Collection?

How long have you been involved?

From your perspective, how has the program helped the seniors in your community?

What would happen if the program didn't exist?

What are some adjectives you would use to describe the program?

INTERVIEW WITH COMMUNITY RELATIONS COORDINATOR

What would you like the Senior Deposit Collection Program to be known for in the larger Ypsilanti community?

Can you recall a time when you learned how the Senior Deposit Collection had an impact on an individual or a group of participants? If so, how?

What difference does the Senior Deposit Collection Program make in the community?

How do you describe the Senior Deposit Collection Program to people inside and outside the library?

How do you currently evaluate the program?

What would you like to know about the program that you don't know now?

INTERVIEW WITH ADULT SERVICES LIBRARIANS

What do you know about the use of the collections?

What kind of follow-up activities do you do (for example, to determine if the books are appropriate)?

Have you ever received thank-you notes?

Do you have any existing data at all that we can examine?

Do you have any plans/ideas for developing the program further?

Have you had much interaction with the seniors themselves? If so, in what way? Can you give an example/story of a specific instance?

Final comments?

INTERVIEW WITH ACTIVITY DIRECTOR AT SENIOR RESIDENTIAL HOME

What do you notice about the collection and how it is used?

How (if at all) have you used the collection in your activities? Or, how has the collection affected your job as activity director?

From your perspective, how do participants benefit from this program? How do you know this?

Can you put yourself in the shoes of a deposit user? What do you think they would say about the program?

Can you recall a time when you learned how the Senior Deposit Collection had an impact on an individual or a group of participants? If so, how?

FOCUS GROUP WITH SENIORS

How do you use the library/collection?

Have you ever used the library books for something other than pleasure reading?

How do you think the library helps or benefits you? Do you feel that having the ability to read books has an impact on your life? Why?

Have you ever talked to others about the library or about what you are reading? If so, what do you tell them?

Can you recall a time when the collection had an impact on yourself or another resident?

How would you feel if the library books weren't available to you?

If you were asked to describe the benefit of the program to another person, what kind of adjectives would you use?

Data Collection and Analysis

Data Collection

As described previously, we felt it important to conduct at least one interview with each center's activity director. In addition, we decided to conduct focus groups with senior residents who use and personally benefit from the books. The activity directors at each center organized the focus groups and selected participants. At the end of our data collection, we had conducted two interviews with one activity director and one interview with the other, and had led two focus groups, each with four female residents. We also decided to interview library staff directly involved in the program. These interviews with the community relations coordinator and the two adult services librarians served primarily to help us understand the context of the program and the library.

Our data collection was based on personal interaction. We looked for outcomes in the words of those directly involved with the program. During interviews and focus groups, we took notes and paid attention to answers. We built on answers given to the general scripted questions with follow-up questions (and, if necessary, additional interviews) that we thought might add helpful data to our research.

In addition, we tried to unobtrusively observe the seniors using library materials and noted any interpersonal interactions sparked by the collection. These observations gave us additional contextual clues as to how the residents use and organize the library, and we were able to glean additional information about the program without having it specifically told to us.

The two residential senior centers analyzed in this study are quite different in both location and living environment. Individually, each one speaks to that center's unique context within the senior deposit program. One center is a new facility, located just outside of town on the campus of a large hospital. Other than the hospital buildings, the surrounding grounds are open, semi-landscaped fields. The library in this senior center is a room located off one of the residential corridors, the door to which is sometimes closed and sometimes open. The room has no windows, but when the lights are on, it is brightly lit. We observed that most seniors who take out and return library books use the checkout sheet provided by the YDL for that purpose. This sheet is maintained by residents who serve on the volunteer-run library committee.

The other residential senior center has been in existence for several years. It is located on a busy urban residential street. It is smaller and more worn than the other residence. The library in this center is located in a large room at the end of one of the main floor hallways. Two of the walls have windows, and a large table in the center is surrounded by several chairs. The library checkout sheet here is empty. Instead, residents take and return books as they please, occasionally passing a book around to other residents if they find it worth recommending. For example, we observed one resident telling another, "put that [book] in my box when you're finished with it."

Data Analysis

At the conclusion of the data collection process, we read all interview transcriptions in detail and agreed on major themes we noticed arising in the data. We then examined the data in increasing detail to identify subthemes and meaning. We considered the frequency of each theme in the data and decided its significance for determining our outcomes. How often is it illustrated in the data? How is it "proved" by output or input? In large part because of our small sample size, we decided not to create a data codebook. Instead, we created an outcomes table (figure 12-2) as a way to organize and analyze the data.

As mentioned earlier, we used other case studies and evaluations found in our literature search in order to enhance our understanding of how to look for patterns in the data.

It should be emphasized that this report is our interpretation of the outcomes based on a limited sample size and time frame. It is not meant to be a complete illustration of the issues and factors facing an outcomes-based study for this type of program and population. Rather, we have drawn from a range of sources to craft an initial outcome framework, and we recommend continued follow-up and analysis.

The Pieces of the Puzzle:
Central, Outward, and Inward Outcomes

The ultimate goal of our data collection and analysis process was to uncover how the senior deposit collection benefited the senior patrons—or how their participation changed what they knew, thought, felt, or were able to do. We discovered three main categories of outcomes: a central outcome; outward outcomes, or those that had an impact on the patrons' relationship to the larger community or society; and inward outcomes, or those that had an impact on the patrons personally.

For purposes of analysis, the outcomes are illustrated in figure 12-1 as a large puzzle with each individual puzzle piece representing a separate category of outcomes. The puzzle can then be divided along its horizontal axis, with the top section representing the outward outcomes and the bottom section the inward ones.

As with any jigsaw puzzle, each piece can stand on its own, but it is in the linking of all pieces that the full picture is portrayed. Not every outcome may be true for each individual patron, but overall the strength of the program comes from the combination and linking of all the pieces of the puzzle.

Central Outcome: Access to Reading

The center piece of the puzzle, or the central outcome, is the linchpin to the program: access to reading. Throughout the course of the study we realized that fundamental to every other program outcome was the fact that the senior deposit collection provided access to books and reading for a population that was losing its access to that resource.

Because of physical limitations and limited mobility, the seniors in these deposit centers have restricted ability to go to the branch libraries. One senior

Figure 12-1 The Outcomes Puzzle

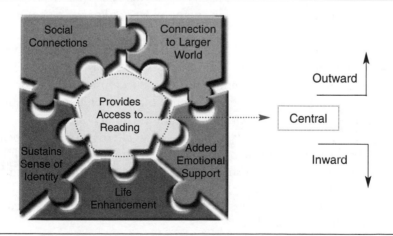

commented, "I can't get to the library. It is really difficult to get in and out of the car." With the deposit collection, however, seniors need only to walk down the hallway to access new and changing reading materials: "It is hard for us to get out sometimes and here the library books are right here."

In addition to restrictions in movement, the seniors we interviewed were experiencing some loss in vision and, as a consequence, appreciated the large-print format of the YDL collection. Overwhelmingly, the seniors commented that large print was much more physically comfortable to read. As one woman told us, "I wouldn't be able to read much of anything if there weren't large-print books available."

Outward Outcomes: Social Connections and Connection to the Larger World

Looking at the top two pieces of the puzzle—social connections and a connection to the larger world—we see the benefits of the program on the patron's relationship to the larger society.

SOCIAL CONNECTIONS

As Hales-Mabry notes, it is not uncommon for older adults to experience a reduction in their social and personal interactions that can contribute to a feeling of isolation.[10] Seniors, especially those who have transitioned into an institutionalized setting, may be experiencing the loss of a previous social network. In addition, many older adults may be coping with the loss of a spouse.

Based on our research, we discovered that the senior deposit collection was aiding seniors in creating both community as well as personal connections. Within their own immediate community, residents formed library committees to provide operational support for the resident library—including circulation, shelving, and collection development. In addition, the library space served as a gathering place for the senior residents, giving them an alternate space for socializing.

The books in the collection were also a common discussion point for residents. Seniors commented on sharing books: "If someone finds a good book, we pass it around." Books were even used as an icebreaker. One resident said, "Sometimes at dinnertime there is a time for people to get acquainted. I always ask people if they use the library."

CONNECTION TO THE LARGER WORLD

In addition to a sense of social isolation, many seniors experience a sense of confinement or of narrowing world viewpoint. However, access to current reading materials help the seniors to reconnect to the larger world. "Reading is a way to not be closed off from the rest of the world. There are lots of benefits to reading, but this is a major one." Furthermore, simply having a library space provides an alternative to their own rooms or apartments, a welcome option for people who have been accustomed to living independently in their own homes.

Inward Outcomes: Identity, Life Enhancement, and Emotional Support

Looking at the bottom three pieces of the puzzle—identity, life enhancement, and emotional support—we can uncover the benefits of the program on the patron's personal well-being and sense of self.

SUSTAINS SENSE OF IDENTITY

Outcomes in the identity category can be further broken down into four subthemes. First, access to the deposit collection seems to give the residents a continued or renewed sense of independence. As these elderly adults move from independent living situations to a more assisted living environment, they do experience some loss of independence. However, having the ability to freely browse the library collection without waiting for a book to arrive in the mail and being able to entertain themselves independent of others' help provides a certain level of autonomy in an environment where they are becoming increasingly dependent on others.

Second, the resident-run libraries give the seniors a sense of control and agency. For example, volunteer residents form library committees and take over the process of organizing the library and shelving the books. From our own observations, we felt this sense of control was an important way that the seniors felt engaged in useful and productive activities.

Third, there was a recognition among those interviewed that reading helped them stay sharp and provided them with "brain food" or mental sustenance. One woman remarked, "It's easy to sit in the corner and not do anything or think anything. Reading helps you get out of that."

Finally, the act of reading and being surrounded by books is a way for the seniors to continue a "normal" type of life—maintaining an activity they enjoyed before moving into the senior residence. Access to library books isn't new to many seniors, and the public library has often been an institution they have called on over the course of their lifetime, so continued access to library books provides security and even a sense of stability.[11] In addition, the act of reading was seen as an everyday and essential part of the residents' lives. It was something they had done their entire lives. One senior said, "I can't imagine not reading."

LIFE ENHANCEMENT

The act of reading gives residents a sense of pleasure and relaxation. One interviewee said, "I couldn't go to sleep without reading." Reading also gives residents an alternative activity or relief from boredom. A senior told us, "Do you know what I do when I get bored? I read poetry." Finally, the frequent rotation of new books gives the residents a sense of excitement or interest. Residents know to look forward to the next drop-off.

ADDED EMOTIONAL SUPPORT

Leisure reading seems to have positive psychological effects for the residents, giving them a sense of escape from some of the problems they might be facing. One senior said, "People who are confined can read and it is a way to get your mind off what is bothering you."

Reading also seems to help the residents cope. One woman wrote us, "As for the library program, I am very interested in that too. At the time I arrived at [the residence home] (one year this month), I was deeply grieving for my husband's passing. I don't know how I could have coped, without the books! They were my salvation. I read dozens this past year, and look forward to the new choice whenever the outreach program brings more."

Areas for Future Study

The outcomes we identified point to the positive impact that the senior deposit collection program has on participating seniors. We also believe our research has unearthed some opportunities to increase the impact of those outcomes.

According to our data, the current system of using checkout sheets for gathering circulation statistics is neither a reliable way to follow what senior residents are reading nor a reliable indication of how many are using the collection. We found that both centers used in this study varied greatly in how they used the checkout sheets. Each center has personalized a method of arranging and maintaining its collection, and this may interfere (or render irrelevant) the data collection framework set up by the YDL.

One area for future study could be to combine the library's need for circulation information and the seniors' need for an active connection between themselves and the greater community. Libraries with senior deposit collections may consider the following.

A recommended reading list or book shelf. Our research indicated that many seniors share books among themselves and, in fact, use them as springboards for conversation and cultivating relationships. A list of recommended books, perhaps displayed on a shelf or table in the library, may help encourage these activities further. The adult services librarians may want to solicit requests for topics from seniors at each center. This could provide a more directed readers advisory service. Perhaps the recommended list could be posted and marked each time one of the books is checked out, giving YDL librarians additional information on how often the books are read.

Enhanced communication between senior centers, initiated by library staff. The nine senior centers served by the program create a default network of patrons. For a population that often feels marginalized or cut off from the greater world, this network offers an untapped opportunity for building meaningful relationships between participating locations. For example, one center's use of the library collection may also be applicable to the activities of another center and encourage it to do something similar. This may be done informally between activity directors and librarians with occasional e-mails, or more formally on a scheduled basis—even by creating an advisory board of senior residents. By facilitating this cross-communication among drop-off locations, YDL librarians would be sharing ideas for how to use the books. In addition to the potential benefits for the seniors, this would also increase the potential reach of the library and its services.

Another area for future study is the need for more artifacts that speak to possible outcomes for these kinds of programs. For this particular study, we relied on interviews, focus groups, and other informal (mostly verbal) communications. Although we were successful, we were ultimately led to the conclusion that relying solely on verbal data collection overlooks powerful opportunities for those hoping to gather outcomes for this kind of program.

For example, we received a letter from a resident at one residential home who found that she was not able to attend our planned focus group. In her place, she sent a letter explaining why she appreciated the library and how it had helped her since arriving at the home. We did not solicit this letter, nor did we suggest that she send us her feedback. This not only told us that she found the program important enough to write, but that for her, writing was the only way she found she could contribute to the study.

To encourage an ongoing collection of artifacts that may help with future outcome-based evaluations, we propose the following ideas for consideration.

Establish a formal feedback procedure. The library may want to use holidays as an opportunity to send cards thanking the seniors for keeping the program successful. If possible, the library may also choose to send along a box of self-addressed, stamped holiday cards, asking the seniors to let them know what books they've liked, if they have any suggestions, or any stories about the library they would like to share. Although this typically may not be successful in many populations, our research indicates that the seniors relish the opportunity and have the time to connect with others outside the senior center.

Create a suggestion box, book, or provide comment slips in books. Another idea for soliciting feedback is for the library to have a suggestion box, feedback book, or comment slips in each library book. This would give seniors a formal opportunity to request library materials and also would give librarians reliable indicators of what the seniors want from the collection. In addition, it is a tangible artifact for the program to reference when evaluating aspects of the program in the future.

These suggestions have not been tested. However, they speak to the outcomes this study has identified, and are attempts to sustain and possibly even enhance those outcomes with a structure that supports further research in this area.

The outcomes achieved by the YDL's senior deposit collection program and the activities and inputs that generated them are given in figure 12-2.

Figure 12-2   Outcomes of the Ypsilanti District Library's
Senior Deposit Collection Program

CENTRAL OUTCOMES
Provides Access to Reading

Outcome: Gives people a chance to read who otherwise wouldn't be able to	Activities	Inputs
Residents able to access library materials without having to physically visit the library:	YDL delivers new and a variety of other books to senior centers every 3 months	Library space made available in each senior center
"It is hard for us to get out sometimes and here the library books are right here."		Organized and physically accessible shelves so residents can get access to the books
"I can't get to the library. It is really difficult for people to get in and out of the car."		Free, unlimited access to rotating library collection. ("These books don't have to be checked out for a limited period of time.")
"I really appreciate them delivering the books."		
Residents have access to large-print books, which are easier to handle:		New, large-print fictional books are circulated every 3 months. ("The books don't sit on the shelves for very long, so there is always something new coming in which keeps it interesting.")
"Having the large print really helps. I can't read small print anymore."		
"I wouldn't be able to read much of anything if there weren't large-print books available."		YDL provides large-print books in new titles to the senior centers
"We rely on the library books because we can read those."		Library staff who participate in book drop-offs
Outcome: Residents learn that the library is a resource	Activities	Inputs
"Some residents don't realize the library is here, so I make sure to tell them."	Active senior residents tell other residents about the library	Comfortable chairs and adequate lighting so residents can read in the library
	Seniors discuss books in social hours or during dinnertime	Library space made available in each senior center

(continued)

Figure 12-2 *(continued)*

Outcome: Residents learn that the library is a resource	Activities	Inputs
		Organized and physically accessible shelves so residents can get access to the books
		Active activity directors who understand and have experience of residents and what they want to read or their interests
		Active residents who utilize the resource

OUTWARD OUTCOMES
Social Connections

Outcome: Provides increased community connections	Activities	Inputs
Residents work together in library committees People know who is on the library committee and seek those people out to request new books The library is a social gathering place	Residents form library committees to keep the books shelved and assist in the circulation process Active senior residents tell other residents about the library Activity directors at some centers have coffee table books available during social hours Residents exchange and talk about books they have read	YDL hands over all circulation and library organization decisions to the senior homes Active residents who utilize the resource Active activity directors who understand and have experience of residents and what they want to read or their interests

Outcome: Provides increased interpersonal connections	Activities	Inputs
"I want to share books that I like." "Sometimes at dinnertime there is a time for people to get acquainted. I always ask people if they use the library." "If we find a good book, it is good to share it with others." "If someone finds a good book, we pass it around." "I talk to people at the dinner table about books." Residents exchange books at the dinner table and talk about them	Activity directors at some centers have coffee table books available during social hours Residents exchange and talk about books they have read	Active residents who utilize the resource Active activity directors who understand and have experience of residents and what they want to read or their interests

Connection to Larger World

Outcome: Access to a wide variety of large-print books allows residents a broadened world viewpoint	Activities	Inputs
"Reading is a way to not be closed off from the rest of the world. There are lots of benefits to reading, but this is a major one." "The books help bring more of the world here to where we are."	YDL delivers new and a variety of other books to senior centers every 3 months YDL adult services staff select books for each deposit center based on feedback from residents or an understanding of the seniors' interests or needs Residents shelve books alphabetically so people can have access	Comfortable chairs and adequate lighting so residents can read in the library Library space made available in each senior center Organized and physically accessible shelves so residents can get access to the books

(continued)

Figure 12-2   *(continued)*

Outcome: Broadening space and reducing sense of confinement	Activities	Inputs
The library space gives residents a place to go other than their rooms/apartments One activity director commented, "Someone is always in the library reading or browsing the books."	YDL delivers new and a variety of other books to senior centers every 3 months Ypsilanti adult services staff select books for each deposit center based on feedback from residents or an understanding of the seniors' interests or needs	Comfortable chairs and adequate lighting so residents can read in the library Library space made available in each senior center Organized and physically accessible shelves so residents can get access to the books

INWARD OUTCOMES
Sustains Sense of Identity

Outcome: Continued or renewed sense of independence	Activities	Inputs
One resident commented, "One man said he could no longer read because his eyesight had gotten so bad that he didn't think he would be able to read for pleasure. But he was able to read the large-print [books in the library]." Residents can entertain themselves independent of others' help: "I would have to rely on my family to bring me books" [if the library collection was not available]. Residents have the freedom to browse the collection and easily exchange one book for another: "If I get home with a book and decide I don't want to read it, I just bring it back to our library and find another one."	Residents read the large-print library books YDL delivers new and a variety of other books to senior centers every 3 months Residents browse the books on the shelf Residents find and choose their own large-print books from the shelf	Library space made available in each senior center Organized and physically accessible shelves so residents can get access to the books Active residents who utilize the resource YDL hands over all circulation and library organization decisions to the senior homes

Outcome: Gives a sense of control and agency	Activities	Inputs
"I love this book my daughter gave me, *How to Become a Late Bloomer*, it is so inspirational. I think more people should read it. I want to start a book group to discuss it." "I don't like pulp romance. But that is all that some women want to read. I don't like looking at them, so I put those books behind the others so they are out of sight." Volunteer residents form library committees and take over the process of organizing the library, shelving the books One activity director said, "The library is a resident-run program. They have ownership of it."	Residents form library committees to keep the books shelved and assist in the circulation process Each day library committee members come in to shelve the books; in fact, they ask that people not shelve the books themselves	YDL hands over all circulation and library organization decisions to the senior homes Active residents who utilize the resource
Outcome: **Mental sustenance**	**Activities**	**Inputs**
"It's easy to sit in the corner and not do anything or think anything. Reading helps you get out of that." Residents are able to easily access a useful way to pass the time: "Reading helps pass the time. Most residents are well aware that they have to use their brain, so reading is a good way to do that." "Without it [the library] I'd feel lost." One activity director said: "Most residents are very well-educated and are used to having information at their fingertips."	Residents read the large-print library books	Free, unlimited access to rotating library collection. ("These books don't have to be checked out for a limited period of time.") New, large-print fictional books are circulated every 3 months. ("The books don't sit on the shelves for very long, so there is always something new coming in which keeps it interesting.")

(continued)

Figure 12-2   *(continued)*

Outcome: Provides a continuation of a normal life or sense of identity	Activities	Inputs
The act of reading and being surrounded by books is a way for the seniors to continue a "normal" type of life—continuing with activities that they enjoyed before they moved out of their homes into a senior residential center. "I was a teacher and always liked books." "I enjoy anything to do with books." A member of the library committee said: "I used to be an executive secretary, I am very organized and like to keep things in place." Reading is an everyday and essential part of the residents' lives. It is something they have done their entire lives. "I can't imagine not reading." "I have to read." "I have always read." One activity director commented: "I think they appreciate the tactile sensation of holding a book, turning the pages. It's familiar." One activity director did an assessment on each of the residents, asking them what their favorite pastimes were. She said that almost all said that they enjoy reading and that it is something that they have done their entire life. "I have always read. I had all of Danielle Steele's books when I was outside."	Residents read the large-print library books Residents find and choose their own large-print books from the shelf YDL delivers new and a variety of other books to senior centers every 3 months Residents form library committees because of lifelong interest in books and reading Residents form library committees to keep the books shelved and assist in the circulation process YDL adult services staff select books for each deposit center based on feedback from residents or an understanding of the seniors' interests or needs	Free, unlimited access to rotating library collection. ("These books don't have to be checked out for a limited period of time.") New, large-print fictional books are circulated every 3 months. ("The books don't sit on the shelves for very long, so there is always something new coming in which keeps it interesting.") YDL provides large-print books in new titles to the senior centers Library staff available to keep in contact with residents and activity directors at each drop-off location Library staff who participate in book drop-offs YDL adult services staff that have experience and an understanding of what residents want to read or are interested in reading Active activity directors who understand and have experience of residents and what they want to read or their interests

Life Enhancement

Outcome: Pleasure	Activities	Inputs
"I read for pleasure most of the time." "Reading helps pass the time." Residents get caught up in the books: "It is sometimes hard to give up reading even to go and eat."	Residents read the large-print library books YDL delivers new and a variety of other books to senior centers every 3 months YDL adult services staff select books for each deposit center based on feedback from residents or an understanding of the seniors' interests or needs YDL looks at circulation statistics to determine book popularity Activity directors give feedback to YDL about residents' reading interests	Free, unlimited access to rotating library collection. ("These books don't have to be checked out for a limited period of time.") New, large-print fictional books are circulated every 3 months. ("The books don't sit on the shelves for very long, so there is always something new coming in which keeps it interesting.") YDL adult services staff who have experience and an understanding of what residents want to read or are interested in reading Active activity directors who understand and have experience of residents and what they want to read or in their interests
Outcome: Relaxation	**Activities**	**Inputs**
"Some people just use the library as a place to relax." "The large-print books are relaxing. I want to read and reading the large print is much more comfortable." "I couldn't go to sleep without reading."	Residents read the large-print library books	YDL provides large-print books in new titles to the senior centers

(continued)

Figure 12-2   *(continued)*

Outcome: Provides a sense of excitement, interest	Activities	Inputs
"There are all kinds of books available when they drop them off. I get surprised how much I enjoy reading them." Residents know to look forward to the next drop-off: "I read dozens this past year, and look forward to the new choice whenever the outreach program brings more." "They bring a wide variety, always something different, always new things to read. New books are something to look forward to."	Residents read the large-print library books YDL delivers new and a variety of other books to senior centers every 3 months YDL adult services staff select books for each deposit center based on feedback from residents or an understanding of the seniors' interests or needs YDL looks at circulation statistics to determine book popularity Activity directors give feedback to YDL about residents' reading interests Residents find and choose their own large-print books from the shelf Library committee members convey other residents' book requests to the YDL	New, large-print fictional books are circulated every 3 months. ("The books don't sit on the shelves for very long, so there is always something new coming in which keeps it interesting.") Library staff available to keep in contact with residents and activity directors at each drop-off location YDL adult services staff that have experience and an understanding of what residents want to read or are interested in reading Active activity directors who understand and have experience of residents and what they want to read or their interests
Outcome: Provides a positive activity or relief from boredom	**Activities**	**Inputs**
Residents volunteer to work on the library committee: "This is really a resident-run program."	Active senior residents tell other residents about the library	Free, unlimited access to rotating library collection. ("These books don't have to be checked out for a limited period of time.")

"Do you know what I do when I get bored? I read poetry."	Residents read the large-print library books Residents form library committees because of lifelong interest in books and reading Residents form library committees to keep the books shelved and assist in the circulation process Seniors discuss books in social hours or during dinnertime	New, large-print fictional books are circulated every 3 months. ("The books don't sit on the shelves for very long, so there is always something new coming in which keeps it interesting.") YDL provides large-print books in new titles to the senior centers Library space made available in each senior center Library staff available to keep in contact with residents and activity directors at each drop-off location Active residents who utilize the resource YDL hands over all circulation and library organization decisions to the senior homes
Outcome: **Provides a sense of escape**	**Activities**	**Inputs**
"We are confined and reading gives us a sense of hope." "It is an escape to be able to read." Residents temporarily forget their problems: "People who are confined can read and it is a way to get your mind off what is bothering you."	Residents read the large-print library books YDL delivers new and a variety of other books to senior centers every 3 months YDL adult services staff select books for each deposit center based on feedback from residents or an understanding of the seniors' interests or needs	Free, unlimited access to rotating library collection. ("These books don't have to be checked out for a limited period of time.") New, large-print fictional books are circulated every 3 months. ("The books don't sit on the shelves for very long, so there is always something new coming in which keeps it interesting.") YDL provides large-print books in new titles to the senior centers

(continued)

Figure 12-2 *(continued)*

Outcome: Provides a sense of escape	Activities	Inputs
	YDL looks at circulation statistics to determine book popularity	Library staff available to keep in contact with residents and activity directors at each drop-off location
	Activity directors give feedback to YDL about residents' reading interests	YDL adult services staff that have experience and an understanding of what residents want to read or are interested in reading
	Residents browse the books on the shelf	Active activity directors who understand and have experience of residents and what they want to read or their interests
	Residents find and choose their own large-print books from the shelf	

Outcome: Aids in coping	Activities	Inputs
"Reading is such a good way to cope. I think if more people could sit down and read, it would really help."	Residents read the large-print library books	YDL adult services staff who have experience and an understanding of what residents want to read or are interested in reading
"It helps us to cope, it is an escape to be able to read."	YDL delivers new and a variety of other books to senior centers every 3 months	Active activity directors who understand and have experience of residents and what they want to read or their interests
One activity director said:		
"Reading is a way for people to pass the time. They have nothing but time and they get bored. It is a way for them to escape into another life."	YDL adult services staff select books for each deposit center based on feedback from residents or an understanding of the seniors' interests or needs	Library staff available to keep in contact with residents and activity directors at each drop-off location
Excerpt of a written letter from one of the senior residents:		Library staff who participate in book drop-offs
"As for the library program, I am very interested in that too. At the time I arrived at—(1 year this month), I was deeply grieving for my husband's passing. I don't know how I could have coped, without the books! They were my salvation.	YDL looks at circulation statistics to determine book popularity	

I read dozens this past year, and look forward to the new choice whenever the outreach program brings more."	Residents find and choose their own large-print books from the shelf	Free, unlimited access to rotating library collection. ("These books don't have to be checked out for a limited period of time.")
		New, large-print fictional books are circulated every 3 months. ("The books don't sit on the shelves for very long, so there is always something new coming in which keeps it interesting.")

NOTES

1. Administration on Aging, U.S. Department of Health and Human Services, *A Profile of Older Americans: 2002* (Washington, D.C.: Department of Health and Human Services, 2002), available at http://research.aarp.org/general/profile_2002.pdf.
2. Reference and User Services Association, "Library Services to Older Adults Guidelines," http://www.ala.org/ala/rusa/rusaprotools/referenceguide/libraryservices.htm.
3. Celia Hales-Mabry, *The World of Aging: Information Needs and Choices* (Chicago: American Library Association, 1993).
4. Betty Turock, ed., *Information and Aging* (Jefferson, N.C.: McFarland, 1988).
5. Turock, ed., *Information and Aging*, 8.
6. Ibid, 7.
7. See Barbara Black, "Outreach Services for Older Adults at the Wadsworth Public Library" (master's research paper, Kent State University, ERIC Document Reproduction Service no. 423 902, 1998); Suzanne Gourlie, "Reading Interests of Older Adult Public Library Users" (master's research paper, Kent State University, ERIC Document Reproduction Service no. 401 931, 1996); Judy Nablo, "Ohio Public Library Services to Older Adults" (master's research paper, Kent State University, ERIC Document Reproduction Service no. 401 920, 1995).
8. United Way, "Introduction to Outcome Measurement: What Are Outcomes?" in "United Way Outcome Measurement Resource Network," http://national.unitedway.org/outcomes/resources/What/intro.cfm.
9. Ypsilanti District Library, "Outreach Services," http://www.hvcn.org/info/ydl/4services/outreach.html.
10. Hales-Mabry, *World of Aging*.
11. Connie Van Fleet, *Public Libraries, Lifelong Learning, and Older Adults: Background and Recommendations* (Washington, D.C.: National Institute on Postsecondary Education, Libraries and Lifelong Learning, Department of Education, 1995), available at http://www.ed.gov/pubs/PLLIConf95/vanfleet.html.

INDEX

A

Accountability
  as benefit of outcome evaluation, 21
  demands for, 4–5
  long-term assessment and, 80–81
Adult Learner Program. *See* New Americans
    Program, Adult Learner Program
Annie E. Casey Foundation, 13–14
Audiences. *See also* Users
  communities and, 73–74
  identification of, 74
  matching with outcomes, 75–76
Audiotaping interviews, 41
Austin (Tex.) Public Library, 18
  Wired for Youth program of, 115, 118
Awards, 21

B

Benefits of libraries
  accountability and, 4
  output measurement and, 5
Benefits of outcome evaluations, 20–22
Bilingual programs. *See* English as a Second
    Language programs
Boulder (Colo.) Public Library, 8
Bowling Alone, 3
Brainstorming
  and determining program impacts, 35
  and selection of measurable outcomes, 87

C

Children's Defense Fund, 12
Chilkoot Indian Association, 116
CIAO program. *See* Community Information
    Agents Online program

CIP. *See* Community Information Program
Circulation
  Hennen American Public Library Rating
    and, 7
  as historical measuring device, 17
Clients. *See* Users
Comment slips, 166
Communication
  as benefit of outcome evaluation, 20–21
  during interviews, 41
  senior population and, 165–66
  shared information and, 142
Communities
  audiences and, 73–74
  Community Information Program and,
    136–46
  data analysis of, 66–67
  library accountability and, 13
  outcome measurements of, 13–15
  teenager involvement in, 18–19
Community brand, 72–73
Community Information Agents Online
    program
  Flint Public Library and, 115–16,
    117–18
  outcomes of, 124–30
  teenagers and, 116
Community Information Program
  database activities, 137–38
  indicators of impact of, 140–41
  information sharing and, 138–39
  outcomes graphic, 80
  outcomes of, 140–49
  publications, 139
  San Mateo County and, 136, 138–40

Community Network User Survey
  follow-up interviews for, 54–56
  survey approach, 51–53
Context
  of Senior Deposit Collection Program,
      154–56

D

Data analysis (qualitative), 65–70
Data collection, 36–63
  focus groups, 38–40
  follow-up interviews, 49–56
  interviews, 40–46
  observation, 47–49
  primary methods of, 38–46
  supplemental methods of, 46–50
Database development, 69–70
  Community Information Program and,
      137–38
Demographics
  data collection plans and, 63
  of Flint, Michigan, 115–16
  and interviewing, 46
  senior population and, 150–51
Disabilities, 90, 137–38
Documentation in data analysis,
      68–69
Dragonfly Project
  Haines Borough Public Library and,
      116–17
  outcomes of, 130–35

E

Edelman, Marian Wright, 12
English as a Second Language programs
  Annie E. Casey Foundation and, 13
  audiences and, 76
  Queens Borough Public Library and, 28,
      42–43, 61–62, 81
  resource allocations and, 82–83
English for Speakers of Other Languages, 28
Environment. *See* Facilities
Equipment
  Dragonfly Project and, 132–35
  interviewing and, 41
ESL programs. *See* English as a Second
      Language programs

Ethnicity and outcome measurements, 16
Evaluations, outcome. *See* Outcome
      evaluations

F

Facilities
  disabled people and, 90
  safety in, 18
Flint (Mich.) Public Library
  Community Information Agents Online
      program and, 115–16, 117–18
Focus groups, 38–40
  data collection plans and, 63
  outcome evaluation and, 17
  and selection of measurable outcomes, 87
Funding
  as benefit of outcome evaluation,
      20–22
  Library Services and Technology Act and,
      88–90

G

Goals
  identification as benefit of outcome
      evaluation, 20
  matching outcomes with, 80–81
Government Results and Performance Act of
      1993, 84
Grant development, 67
Graphic outcome representations, 78–80

H

Haines (Alaska) Borough Public Library
  Dragonfly Project and, 117–18
HAPLR. *See* Hennen American Public Library
      Rating
Hartford (Conn.) Public Library, 7–8
Health information services, 16
Health Services Agency, 139
Hennen American Public Library Rating, 7
Hernon, Peter, 21
HLLH outcome model. *See* How Libraries and
      Librarians Help outcome model
How Libraries and Librarians Help outcome
      model, 16–18
  contextual factors, 25–30

I

IMLS. *See* Institute of Museum and Library
    Services
Immigrant populations. *See also* English as a
    Second Language programs
    achievement of personal gains for, 79
    outcomes for, 19, 28–29
    resource allocations and, 82–83
Information Behavior in Everyday Contexts, x
Information sharing, 142
Information/referral services, 16
Institute of Museum and Library Services, 4–5
    benefits of outcome evaluations and, 21
    Dragonfly Project and, 116–19
    How Libraries and Librarians Help out-
        come model and, 16–18
Internet. *See* Technology
Interviews, 40–46
    Community Network User Survey, 51–53
    follow-up, 49–56
    outcome evaluation and, 17
    and selection of measurable outcomes, 87
    Senior Deposit Collection Program and,
        157–59
    Washtenaw Literacy and, 97–98

L

Libraries
    accountability of, 4–5
    contributions of, 3–4
Library models, 88–90
Library Services and Technology Act, 88–90
Literacy. *See also* English as a Second
    Language programs
    data collection plans and, 63
    impact of, 29–30
    Project Literacy Victoria and, 15
    Washtenaw Literacy and, 93–113
Los Angeles Public Library, 90
LSTA. *See* Library Services and Technology Act

M

Marin (Calif.) County Library, 88–89
Marketing, 72–73
    English as a Second Language programs
        and, 28
    vehicles for, 75, 77

Mission statements, 5–6
Mobile library, 89–90

N

*National Survey of Public Library Services for
    Older Adults* (1971), 152
Networking
    as benefit of outcome evaluation, 21
    Community Information Program and,
        138–39
    Senior Deposit Collection Program and,
        162–63, 168–69
New Americans Program, Adult Learner
    Program. *See also* English as a Second
    Language programs
    activities, 28
    data collection methods, 41–46
    data collection plan, 61–62
    outcomes graphic, 79
    resource allocation plan, 82

O

Observation, 47–49
Open-ended questions, 56–61
Outcome evaluations. *See also* Outcomes
    benefits of, 20–22
    of Community Information Agents Online
        program, 124–30
    of Community Information Program,
        141–49
    and documentation, 68–69
    of Dragonfly Project, 133–35
    feedback procedures and, 166
    graphic representations of, 78–80
    How Libraries and Librarians Help out-
        come model and, 24–30
    matching audience with, 75–76
    program improvements due to, 81
    resource allocations and, 82–83
    of Senior Deposit Collection Program,
        151–53, 160–64
    and strategic planning, 22
    of Washtenaw Literacy, 99–113
    of Wired for Youth program, 119–24
Outcome studies
    determining data collection methods for,
        36–37. *See also* Data collection

Outcome studies (*continued*)
  preparing to determine program impacts,
    33–35
Outcomes, 12–22. *See also* Outcome evalua-
    tions
  benefits of evaluation of, 20–22
  categories of, 13–15
  How Libraries and Librarians Help model
    of, 16–17
  predicting, 84–90
Outcomes Toolkit, x
Output measures, 6–8
  Hennen American Public Library Rating
    and, 7
  for How Libraries and Librarians Help out-
    come model, 26–30
  library accountability and, 4–5
  as planning tool, 84–88
Output Measures for Public Libraries, 6–7
Outreach programs for disabled people, 90

P
Patrons. *See* Users
Peninsula (Calif.) Library System, 136
  Community Information Program and,
    139–40
*Perspectives on Outcome Based Evaluation for
    Libraries and Museums*, 21
Planning
  for marketing, 77
  outcome measures and, 84–88
  Public Library Association and, 6
  strategic, 22
Primary data collection methods, 38–46
Project Literacy Victoria, 15
Providence (R.I.) Public Library, 5
  and testimonials, 8–10
Public Library Association, 6
Putnam, Robert, 3

Q
QBPL. *See* Queens (N.Y.) Borough Public
    Library
Qualitative data analysis, 65–70. *See also* Data
    collection
Queens (N.Y.) Borough Public Library
  data collection plan for, 61–62

  and graphic representations, 78–80
  and interviewing, 41–46
  New Americans Program of, 28
  preparing to determine program impacts,
    34–35

R
Reading list, 165
Resource allocation, 82–83, 143
Ross, Janet, 72
Rudd, Peggy, 4, 21

S
San Diego (Calif.) County Public Law
    Library, 89
San Mateo (Calif.) County, 136,
    138–40
Seiss, Judith, 73
Senior Deposit Collection Program
  and areas for future study, 165–66
  data collection/analysis and, 159–60
  outcomes of, 160–64, 167–77
  study design of, 154–59
  Ypsilanti District Library and, 153
Sheppard, Beverly, 21
South San Francisco Public Library, 13
Staff
  as contextual factor in How Libraries and
    Librarians Help outcome model,
    26–27
  of Flint Public Library, 117
  of Haines Public Library, 117
  and interviewing, 41–43
  monitoring outcomes by, 70
  and selection of measurable outcomes, 87
  targeting outcomes to audiences by,
    73–74
  of Washtenaw Literacy, 95–96
Stanford Public Information and Retrieval
    System, 137
Stories and testimonials, 8–10, 18
Strategic planning, 22
Suggestion box, 166
Supplemental data collection methods, 46–50
Surveys
  Community Network User Survey, 51–56
  outcome evaluation and, 17

T
Technology
Community Information Agents Online program and, 115
Dragonfly Project and, 116
Wired for Youth program and, 115
youth technology programs, 114–35
Teenagers
community technology programs and, 114–19
outcome measurements and, 16, 18–19
Theme identification in data analysis, 66–67
Training
for outcome evaluation, 20
for volunteers, 96
Tuolumne County (Calif.), 89–90
Tutors. *See also* Volunteers
Washtenaw Literacy and, 96–98, 112

U
United Way
benefits of outcome evaluations and, 20
outcome model of, 24
and use of outcomes as measurements, 13–14
Users
Community Information Program and, 139–40
as contextual factor in How Libraries and Librarians Help outcome model, 25, 27
and determining program impacts, 34–35
focus groups for, 38–40
interviews with, 43–46
open-ended questions for, 56–61

public library youth technology programs and, 114–19
qualitative data analysis and, 65
Washtenaw Literacy and, 96

V
The Visible Librarian: Asserting Your Value with Marketing and Advocacy, 73
Vital Signs Project, 14–15
Volunteers
and selection of measurable outcomes, 87
Washtenaw Literacy and, 95–96

W
Washtenaw Literacy, 93–113
basic findings for, 99–101
contextual factors affecting, 94–96
data collection methods and analysis, 96–99
outcomes of, 99–112
Websites
of Outcomes Toolkit, x
use in evaluations, 94
WFY program. *See* Wired for Youth program
Wired for Youth program
Austin (Tex.) Public Library and, 115
focus group guide, 39–40
outcomes of, 119–24
youth and, 118

Y
Ypsilanti (Mich.) District Library
Senior Deposit Collection Program and, 153
Washtenaw Literacy and, 93

Joan C. Durrance has authored scores of articles and several books that focus on people's need for information and the methods that libraries use to increase their access to it, particularly community-focused approaches. Her most recent book, coauthored with Karen Fisher (formerly Karen Pettigrew), is *Online Community Information: Creating a Nexus at Your Library* (2001). Her writings are based on a number of studies, several of them funded by the Institute of Museum and Library Services (IMLS). This research seeks to help librarians better understand the information-seeking behavior of consumers and identify best practices in the provision of community information services. Durrance holds the rank of professor at the University of Michigan's School of Information.

Karen E. Fisher (née Pettigrew) is an assistant professor at the Information School of the University of Washington, where she teaches information behavior, community analysis, and quantitative research methods. She holds a Ph.D. in library and information science (1998) from the University of Western Ontario. She has published the results of her research in numerous articles and has served as co-principal investigator with Joan Durrance on several recent IMLS-funded projects.